1. Jarawa Young Couple

2. Jarawa Girl

3. Friendly Contact with Jarawas: Gifts on the Beach

4. An Onge Couple

5. A Normal Life of Shompen Women

6. A Marvelous Sun Set: A View from Junglighat

7. An Orchid Flower

8. Monitor Lizards of Andamans

9. Spotted Deers of Andamans

10. Shri Vetrimalai Murugan Temple

11. An Ariel View of Port Blair City

12. All wings of Cellular Jail

13. A Workshop for convicts inside the Cellular Jail.

14. Andaman Water Sports Complex

15. Adventure Water Sports in the Andaman Water Sports Complex

16. An Ariel View of Andaman Water Sports Complex

17. An Ariel View of Gandhi Park

18. Marina Park

19. Carbyns Cove Beach

20. Gymkhana Ground Swimming Pool

21. A Beautiful Sun Rise at Wandoor Beach

22. Cinque Island Beach

23. Jollybouy Island Beach

24. Volcanic Barran Island

25. Tourist Home, Haddo - Port Blair

26. Andaman Teal House, Dilanipur - Port Blair

PORT BLAIR TOWN MAP
SERVICES
1 INDIAN AIRLINES
2 SHIPPING CO OF INDIA
3 MARINE & SHIPPING
4 TOURISM OFFICE SECRETARIAT
5 RAJ-NIVAS
6 G.B. PANT HOSPITAL
7 BUS TERMINUS
8 HEAD POST OFFICE
9 TELEGRAPH OFFICE
10 GOVT. COLLEGE
11 ABERDEEN P.S.
12 STATE BANK OF INDIA
13 SYNDICATE BANK
14 CANARA BANK
15 GYMKHANA GROUND
16 TRANSPORT OFFICE
17 FERRY BOOKING/ PHOENIXBAY JETTY
18 STATE LIBRARY
19 GOVT. OF INDIA TOURIST OFFICE
20 HADDO JETTY
21 AIRPORT & TOURIST INFORMATION CENTRE
22 SAGAR TOURS AND TRAVELS
23 SHOMPEN TRAVELS
24 ISLAND TRAVELS
LODGING
25 TOURIST HOME/ MEGAPODE NEST
26 GUEST HOUSE NO. 1
27 CORBYN'S COVE GUEST HOUSE
28 HORNBILL NEST
29 MARINE HILL NOOK NEST
30 MUNICIPAL GUEST HOUSE, D/PUR
31 BAY ISLAND HOTEL
32 ANDAMAN BEACH RESORT
33 SINCLAIRS BAY VIEW
34 N.K. INTERNATIONAL
35 HOTEL DHANALAKSHMI
36 HOTEL SHOMPEN/TRAVELS
37 HOTEL SHALIMAR
38 HOTEL ABHISHEKH
39 HOTEL KAVITHA
40 HOTEL BENGAL K.P.
TOURIST SPOTS
41 CELLULAR JAIL NATIONAL MEMORIAL
42 ANTHROPOLOGICAL MUSEUM
43 FISHERIES MUSEUM
44 CORBYN'S COVE BEACH
45 CHATHAM SAW MILL
46 MINI ZOO
47 MARINA PARK
48 DILTHAMAN TANK
49 COTTAGE INDUSTRIES EMPORIUM
50 ZOOLOGICAL MUSEUM
51 FOREST MUSEUM

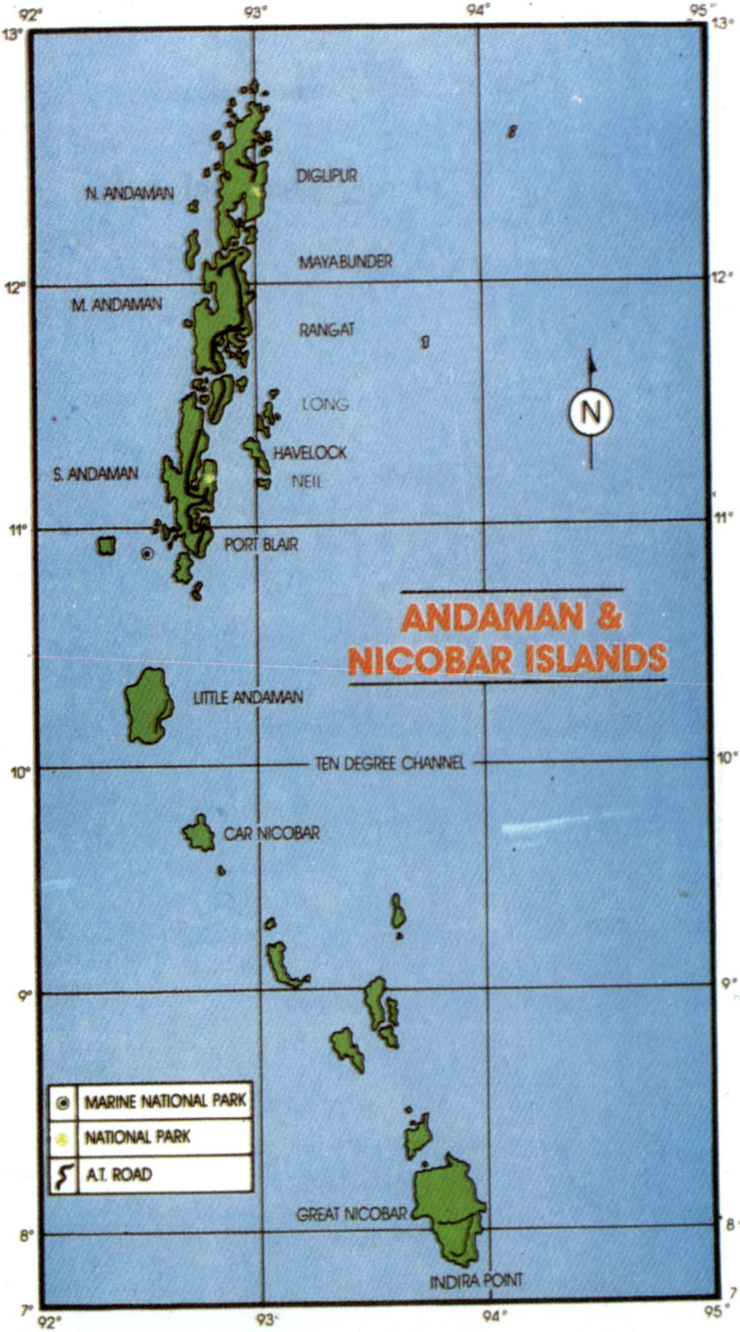
ANDAMAN & NICOBAR ISLANDS
N. ANDAMAN
DIGLIPUR
MAYABUNDER
M. ANDAMAN
RANGAT
LONG
HAVELOCK
NEIL
S. ANDAMAN
PORT BLAIR
LITTLE ANDAMAN
TEN DEGREE CHANNEL
CAR NICOBAR
GREAT NICOBAR
INDIRA POINT
MARINE NATIONAL PARK
NATIONAL PARK
A.T. ROAD
N
92°
93°
94°
95°
13°
12°
11°
10°
9°
8°
7°

Tourism
In
Andaman and Nicobar Islands

Tourism

In

Andaman and Nicobar Islands

Dr. N. Rajavel

MANAS PUBLICATIONS
New Delhi - 110002 (INDIA)

MANAS PUBLICATIONS
(Publishers, Distributors, Importers & Exporters)
4402/5-A, Ansari Road (Opp. HDFC Bank)
Darya Ganj, New Delhi - 110 002 (India)
Phones: Off.: 011-23260783, 23265523,
Res.: 011-23842660
E-mail: manaspublications@gmail.com
www.manaspublications.in

ISBN: 978-81-7049-087-6 (13 Digits)
81-7049-087-1 (10 Digits)

Rs. 500/-

Designed at
Manas Publications
Printed in India at
RK Print Services, Delhi
and published by Mrs Suman Lata for
Manas Publications, 4402/5-A,
Ansari Road (Opp HDFC Bank),
Darya Ganj, New Delhi - 110002 (INDIA)

Preface

Travel has, now-a-days, become a social necessity. The modern transport, paid holidays, leave travel concessions, reservation facilities, eagerness to know about different kinds of civilizations, cultures, importance of the place etc. are the main reasons for such travel. Tourism was regarded once as a luxury and that too, reserved for a certain group of people. But the trend has completely changed now. Every one has realised the significance of tourism as a source of income, employment and a major factor for the economic development and now that the tourism is no longer a luxury.

A & N Islands has vast vital resources and potentialities for the development of tourism which perhaps no other part of the mainland of India and for that matter no other country in the world has because of its special geographical location, her lush green scenic beauty, historical importance, multilingual cultural heritage, colourful cultural life, its being a symbol of National Integration, harmonious life, customs and social life, fairs and festivals, tribal culture etc. Due to the location of these islands, the tourism in these islands of mari-gold sun of Bay of Bengal has high scope with a lot of tourism resources. But the A & N Islands has not been able to attract the tourists even to the Break Even Level, and hence this piece of work.

This book covers almost all aspects of Tourism in Andaman and Nicobar Islands in nine chapters. Chapter 1 is Introduction. Chapter 2 is related to the Profile of A & N Islands. Chapter 3 deals with the Population; Chapter 4 discusses the Tourism Attractions and Chapter 5 is about the Tourism Facilities available in Islands. Chapter 6 deals with the Growth of Tourism in these islands. Chapter 7 emphasises the views and satisfaction expressed by the tourists about the tourism attractions and facilities available in this territory. Chapter 8 focuses on the problems of Tourism. Chapter 9 gives the suggestions for Planning Tourism and Development of Tourism in the lush green paradise. This book is written in very simple language. It is very useful for Govt. Authorities, Agencies, Planners, Administrators Tour Operators, Travelling Agents, Tourist Offices, Educational Institutions, Researchers, Hoteliers and all those interested in tourism and the tourists.

My first and foremost sincere thanks to Dr. R.M. Saksena, Professor, Head and Dean, Faculty of Commerce, Kumaun University, Nainital for his continuous encouragement. I express my grateful thanks to the Department of Tourism, A & N Administration, Port Blair, Adim Jan Jathi Vikas, Port Blair, Indian Airlines, Port Blair, Census Office, Port Blair, ANIIDCO, Port Blair, Municipal Council, Port Blair, all private lodge owners, all hoteliers, taxi and car owners, tour operators etc. who have given the required data for this book.

Also I express my sincere gratitude to all tourists who have filled up the questionnaires, officers of the different offices who have given their valuable time in filling up of the questionnaires, in discussion etc. I am equally indebted to many individuals, organisations who have provided necessary information from time to time and were generous with their time and contribution. I am obliged to New Prabhat Studio, Delanipur, Port Blair for processing some photographs.

Also my sincere thanks to Mr. Suresh, Mrs. Suresh and Mr. Raj SBI, Mr. Ramachandran, Miss Sumitra, Miss Sitara, Mr. Prakash, Mr. Vasu, Miss Rekha, Mr. Prakash, for their valuable cooperation in computer corrections and typing; Mr. Santosh Kumar for the graphs and diagrams. I am no less indebted to all my friends and well wishers who have very kindly extended their help to me at every crucial stage. Also I express my gratitude to Sh. V.K. Garg, Manas Publications who has made the present work to see the light of the day.

N. Rajavel

Contents

List of Photographs

Important Telephone Numbers (STD Code: 03192)

Indian Airlines Booking Office	:	33108
Airport	:	32983 & 32272
East West Airlines Booking Office	:	30935 & 32945
Shipping Corporation of India	:	33347
Directorate of Shipping	:	33180
Tourism Office	:	32747 & 32694
Govt. of India Tourist Office	:	33006
Port Blair Bus Terminal	:	32278
Head Post Office	:	32226
Head Telegraphic Office	:	32551
G.B. Pant Hospital Complex	:	32102
All India Radio	:	32363 & 30118
The Daily Telegrams(daily)	:	32810
Andaman Herald(daily)	:	30171 & 33222
Power House	:	32786
Police Head Quarters	:	33077 & 32100
Aberdeen Police Station	:	33077
Netaji Stadium	:	32398
Andaman Water Sports Complex	:	30799
Cellular Jail, National Memorial	:	32759
Cellular Jail, L & S Show	:	33388
Anthropological Museum	:	32291
Fisheries Museum	:	32719
Carbyn's Cove Complex	:	32043
Airport Aerodrom Officer	:	33390
Gandhi Park	:	30898

Hotels and Guest Houses

		Telephone Nos.
Tourist Home Complex	:	32380
Megapot Nest	:	32207
Andaman Teal House	:	32642
Circuit House	:	32750
Hornbill Nest	:	32018
Youth Hostel	:	32459
Bay Island Hotel	:	32881
Peerles Resort	:	33462 & 33464
Sinclair's Bay View	:	32973 & 33159
Hotel Shompen	:	32360 & 32425
Hotel Abhishek	:	33565
Hotel N.K. International	:	33066
Hotel Dhanalakshmi	:	33953
Hotel Shalimar	:	33923
Hotel Kavitha	:	33742
Ram Nivas Lodge	:	33217
Tourist Cottage	:	33021
Shompen Lodge	:	32425
Sampat Lodge	:	33752
Hotel Bengal KP	:	32964
Rathan Lodge	:	32133
Sagar Alok Lodge	:	33587
Jaganath Guest House	:	33140
Anand Lodge	:	33252
Central Lodge	:	33632 & 33634
Phoniex Lodge	:	33820
Holiday Resort	:	30516

Andaman and Nicobar Islands At a Glance

Status	:	Union Territory in India
Location	:	Bay of Bengal
Geographical Situation	:	Longitude : 92° to 94° East Latitude : 6° to 14° North Altitude : 732 Mts.
Area	:	Andamans : 6408 Sq. Kms. Nicobars : 1841 Sq. Kms. A & N Is. : 8249 Sq. Kms.
Name of the Capital	:	Port Blair with City Status
Distance By Sea with Capital	:	From Chennai - 1190 Kms. From Calcutta - 1255 Kms. From Visakhapatnam - 1200 Kms.
Population	:	Andamans - 241453 Nicobars - 39208 A & N Is. - 280661 Male - 154369 Female - 126292 **Total - 280661** Urban - 74955 Rural - 205708 Density - 34 Per
Sq.Km.		
		Sex Ratio - 818 per 1000 Males
Climate 3180(mm)	:	Normal Annual Rain fall
		Mean Temp. - Maximum 30.2° C Mean Temp. - Minimum 23.8° C Mean Relative Humidity - 79%
Monsoons	:	Two (South West and North East)
Tourist Season	:	From October to May
Administrative Divisions	:	Districts : Two Sub Divisions : Four Tehsils : Seven Trade Regions : Eight
Literacy Rate	:	73.02%
Shops & Commercial Establishments	:	922

ANDAMAN AND NICOBAR ISLANDS, INDIA

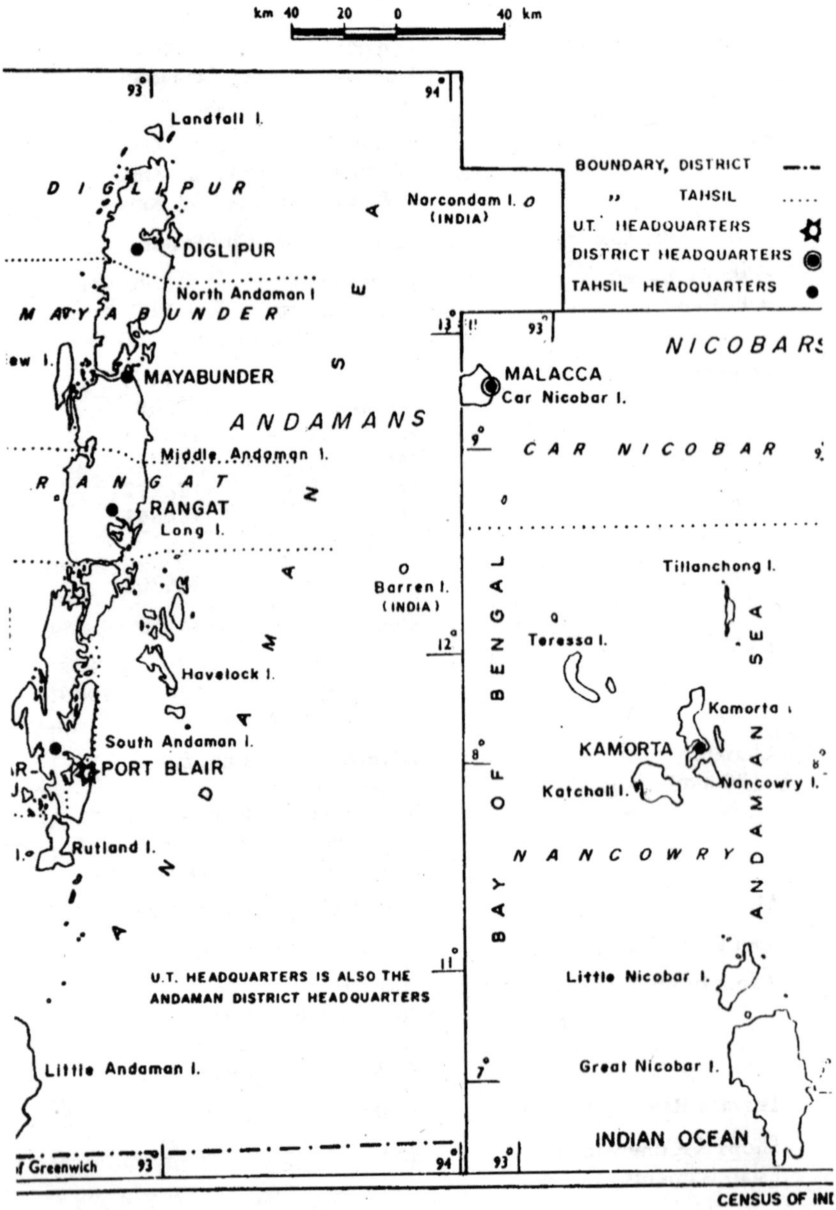

1

INTRODUCTION

Travel is an ancient phenomenon. Reasons for why man travels are plenty. In the early past of human history, man travelled to satisfy his biological needs whereas during the subsequent periods, he travelled for socio-political, religious and economic purposes. Fast expansion of means of travel, namely aircraft fleets, ships and boats, efficient communication system, improved accommodation, the leisure time and paid holidays are some of the important reasons as to why people travel. Moreover, the improvement in the tourism facilities like introduction of flights, connecting services, chartered ships, cheaper accommodation have further stimulated the satisfactory sophisticated travel. Whether a particular travel is tourism or not depends upon the length of journey one undertakes. Tourism necessarily involves longer journey from one place to another. Besides the length and purpose of journey are also other aspects to be taken into account. Some travel for pleasure, some for education, and others for business etc, and hence it is difficult to distinguish and identify the purpose in concrete terms.

Definition of Tourism

A crystal clear concept and a precise definition of tourism is necessary for different purposes. It is, therefore, necessary to describe and define what "tourism" covers. Many authors have given their own definitions of tourism. Of these, a widely accepted definition is the one given by the International Union of Official Travel Organisation (IUOTO), popularly known as World Tourism Organisation (WTO). This definition covers :

1. "Tourists who are temporary visitors staying for at least 24 hours in the country visited and the purpose of whose journey can be classified under one of the following headings :
   (a) Leisure (recreation holidays, health, study, religion and sport
   (b) Business, family, mission, meeting.
2. Excursionists who are temporary visitors staying for less than 24 hours in the country visited, including travellers on cruise ship".

Another definition, given by eminent Swiss Professors, Hunziker and Krapt, is "Tourism is the sum of phenomenon and relationship arising from the travel and stay of non-residents in so far as they do not lead to permanent residence and are not connected with any earning activity". This definition was subsequently adopted by International Association of Scientific Experts in Tourism (AIEST). As per the definition there are three distinct elements of tourism.

1. Involvement of travel
2. Stay of temporary nature in the area visited
3. Stay not connected with any activity involving earnings.

According to Bukart and Medliq, "Tourism denotes the temporary and short term movement of people to destinations outside the place where they normally live and work and their activities at those destinations". So, by taking a view of the above definitions and the geographical location of Andaman and Nicobar (A&N) Islands, available transport facilities to these islands, "Tourism", for present study, is defined as the inflow of people on short term travel from the mainland of India and abroad into one island from the other islands and staying there, at least, one night without any earning motivation.

Tourism as an Industry

Industry plays an important role in the economy of any country. Growth of industrial sector is the parameter to measure the economic development of a country particularly the developing country like that of India. Tourism is now rightly added to the long list of established industries. It has tremendous economic and social potentiality because it generates income and employment opportunities, particularly foreign exchange which is earned more easily and brought in by the tourist himself to his destination. The contribution of this tourism industry to the regional development of the trade, commerce and manufacturing sectors, tax revenue to the government and the national income of the country as a whole is undisputed. It is mainly a labour intensive industry, providing employment to the semi-skilled and the unskilled. For example, as per the cost benefit study of tourism, made by the National Council of Applied Economic and Resarch, New Delhi, tourism generated employment for 934000 persons in 1972-73. This figure rose to 64,09,000 in 1978. This increase in employment stimulates education at different levels. The newly created jobs demand a special schooling and subsequently the standard of general education as a whole comes to a higher level.

In 1929 the world travel revenues were estimated at 30,000 million dollars which worked out to 2% of world product. By 1979, this amount rose to 450 thousand dollar which is about 6% of world product. These figures speak of the growth and importance of the tourism industry. Besides generating income and employment opportunities, the development in tourism gives an impetus to social relationships. The tourism industry plays a positive role in the field of both inter-state and international relationships. It brings about regional as well as international understanding. Tourism industry brings and joins the people of different cultures, religions, languages, etc. Thus it provides them an opportunity to share their ideas which is very important to all countries.

In 1990 the number of world travellers was 429 million and they spent over US $ 249 billions. Direct employment in tourism industry was 112 million and the indirect was much more. In India, the number of domestic tourists was estimated at 62.3 million in 1990. Foreign tourists, in the country during the same period were 1.71 million who spent Rs. 2440 crore in terms of foreign exchange. During 1991-92, the foreign exchange earnings were about Rs. 3500 crore. During 1989-90, the tourism industry in India generated direct employment of 5.5 million persons and another 8 millions were employed indirectly.

Tourism Industry in A & N Islands

The union territory of A&N Islands has realised the importance of tourism in this nature's gifted paradise. Efforts have been made to declare this economic activity as industry as per recommendations of the Ministry of Tourism, Government of India. With a view to developing the tourism in Andaman & Nicobar Islands, it has been decided to treat 'Tourism' as an industry in the Union Territory. This will enable those engaged in tourism and promotional activities in A & N Islands to become eligible for concessions/incentives as applicable to the economic industrial sector from time to time wherever such schemes are relevant to tourism activities.

The following concessions are made available to the tourism sector under relevant schemes operated by different departments such as industry, transport and education, etc.

1. Subsidy for preparation of feasibility/project report.
2. Investment subsidy as applicable from time to time.
3. Incentives for training for local manpower.
4. Augmenting availability of funds from state's financial corporations.
5. Concessions in electricity and water charges.
6. Allocation of land at concessional rate.

7. Exemption from building tax levied by the Revenue Department/Municipal Corporation.

Concessions are also given to and made available to classified hotels, restaurants, purchase of luxury cars, coaches and boats etc., by tour operators, construction of amusement parks, recreation centres, auditoriums, handicrafts emporiums, rope ways, institutions teaching surfing, ski-ing, trekking, etc.

A & N Islands are rich in resources for tourism which are found in abundance. The natural beauty of the Islands is very attractive which often urges the writers to term them as the Green Islands in the Marigold sun. They are now being recognised as tourists' paradise by both the domestic and foreign tourists. The expanse of A & N Islands is everywhere sparkingly beautiful. The surrounded waters are studded in many directions with numerous hillocks, rocks and islets, many of them exceedingly pretty and picturesque with marvellous green oasis in the Bay of Bengal.

A most hospitable and cosmopolitan society, free from rigidity of caste, creed and religion, projecting composite Indian culture, A & N islands are characterised by unity in diversity. The undulating terrain, the inter-play of land, sea and serpentine creeks, the bright white trips of the sun-kissed sea beaches, the blue bays, the rich tropical forests fringed by bright green mangroves, all combine to enhance the scenic value of the Islands in a way not to be found anywhere else in the country. The green vegetation and back waters etc. altogether make the Islands most serene and enchanting.

There are about 1200 industrial units in A & N Islands. All these are wood and marine based, etc. But the industrial development in the islands has not been fast enough. Though the population growth is quite high, better improvement in literacy rate, provision for incentives and concessions, subsidies, and bounties can prove a big help to the industrialists. Hence the tourism industry, along with the other allied activities like trade and commerce needs attention of the administration, planners, policy makers, hoteliers, economists, researchers, academicians and tour operators to find out ways and means to improve the tourism facilities by reducing the transport fares both for ships as well as for flights in terms of different socio cultural and economic, and marketing indicators so that, tourism in these islands can reach the vast majority of population. This requires effective planning and a detailed study of the available resources favourable to the tourism industry in this territory.

Objectives of the Present Work

The major and the main objectives of the present work are as under:

i) to highlight the profile of A & N Islands including population,

ii) to identify the natural and man made tourist resources in these islands,

iii) to study the existing tourist facilities in these islands,

iv) to trace the growth of tourism in the islands by taking into account both foreign and domestic tourism during plan periods and total amount of money invested on tourism industry by the A & N administration,

v) to analyse the tourism data with a view to find out the problems facing tourism, and

vi) to offer suitable suggestions for the planning and development of tourism in A & N islands.

Multiplier Effect

Tourism industry occupies an important place in the natural income of a country. The inflow of money, generated by receipts from the tourists' spending, multiplies as it passes through various sections of economy. The actual income from the tourism sector cannot be measured because of the multiplier effect which is an income concept. The multiplier has been defined by the eminent economists like Khan and Keynes. Their theory can be explained in a simple way that an initial investment or expenditure of tourists makes or gives some primary effects like income or savings, etc. These primary effects also produce some secondary effects of the same type as the first and so on. This process is repeated several times in a given period of time. This creates a chain reaction in the economy. In other words, the money spent by a tourist is, automatically, being circulated through the economy by stimulating itself frequently. Of course, the value of tourism multipler cannot be the same for every country. It varies from nation to nation, depending upon the state of economy. According to Khan and Keynes, the formula for tourism multiplier which is denoted by " K " is,

$$K = \frac{1}{MPS + MPI}$$

Where MPS stand for Marginal Propensity to Save;

Where MPI stands for Marginal Propensity to Import.

As per the above farmula, it is possible to calculate the sum of various primary, secondary and teritiary effects of the same type and hence the relation between the total effect of the same nature and the primary effect and with the help of multiplier the total effect can be calculated.

Tourism Resources

The resources of tourism industry in A & N islands are broadly divided into two kinds-natural resources and man made resources. The natural resources include scenic beauty, climate, flora, fauna etc., and the man made resources include national, memorial, religious and cultural resources, fairs and festivals, commercial and industrial units, sports facilities, shopping, etc. These are discussed in detail in the respective chapters

Tourism Data

The data has been collected for the purpose of this present work from the tourism department, Indian Airlines, private lodge owners, tour operators, transport department, shipping department, entreprenuers, banks, hotels, and from the general public. This data have been grouped and analysed. To find out the level of satisfaction, dissatisfaction and views of tourists about the tourism facilities in A & N islands, the data has been collected from the domestic and foreign tourists by selecting samples through random sampling technique along with questionnaires. All the data, primary as well as secondary, have been analysed, interpreted with ratio techniques and presented in the present form.

2

ANDAMAN AND NICOBAR ISLANDS - A PROFILE

Andaman and Nicobar Islands, by virtue of their strategic geographical location in the Bay of Bengal and rich natural resources, attract and receive great attention. The Bay Islands, as they are also known, constitute the remotest region of our country. The inky, blue waters of the Bay of Bengal and the Andaman Sea, once coined as KALAPANI (the black water) indicating the dreaded transportation, punishment of the British Government of India and the overwhelming grandeur of vast, cloud-ridden skies make them a domain of unsullied nature. "KALAPANI" is all that many have heard of is a term that for centuries conjured up the dark vision of forbidden land surrounded by vast sheets of deep water, unapproachable and hostile. The inhabitants of these islands are scattered far flung and wide over a distance of 720 kms. Some of them are found established well in a few towns and innumerable small villages. But due to the location of these small villages, inhabitants are cut-off from civilisation and from the source of supply of essential commodities. The towns and small villages have started flourishing only recently because of the harbour facilities that have been provided in these islands and slow progress of shipping and other transport facilities. Andaman and Nicobar islands are a green paradise which stretches its long arm of welcome to the mainland across the sea, an outpost pulsating some pioneering activities.

A&N Islands are situated in the Bay of Bengal and located between 6 degree and 14 degree of North latitude and 92 degree and 94 degree of East longitude. This, surrounded by Burma, Thailand, Malaysia, and Indonesia, constitutes the most isolated part of the Indian Union, stretching in a north-south direction, separated from the mainland of India by vast stretches of sea. The islands of this territory are a part of the continuous ridge that extends from Cape Nagrais in Burma through Cocoa Islands and continue further south upto Sumatra. The southern most tip of the territory is Indira Point (previously named as Pigmilion Point) in Great Nicobar which is only 146 kms. distant from Sumatra. These islands comprise two separate groups, namely, the Andaman group of Islands and the Nicobar group of islands with entirely different population and problems. The Andaman group of islands is separated from Nicobar group of Islands by the boisterous 10 degree channel. The said 10 degree channel is about 145 kms. wide and 400 fathoms deep. The location of Andaman & Nicobar Islands is in the Bay of Bengal. The seat of administration is at Port Blair, the Capital of Andaman & Nicobar Islands which is connected with Calcutta by a sea distance of 1225 kms. and with Chennai by 1191 kms. and with Vishakapatnam by 1200 kms.

A&N Islands comprising an area of 8293 sq.kms. are a group of picturesque islands. The Andaman group including the Richie Archipelago stretches over 46 kms. in length and has a maximum breadth of 51 kms., the average width being only 24 kms. The land area of Andaman group is 6340 sq.kms. Some 258 islands, large and small, constitute Andaman. Of these, North Andaman, Interview Islands, Middle Andaman, South Andaman, Little Andaman, Rutland etc., are large islands and hundred islands are yet to be named. The Nicobar group covers 293 kms. between furthest point, the width being 57 kms. The total land area of Nicobar group of Islands is 1953 sq.kms. As many as 61 Islands, large and small, make up the Nicobars, of which Car Nicobar, Teressa, Kamorta, Nancowry, Katchal, Little Andaman and Great Nicobar are large islands and 33 remain unnamed. In this group, the Great Nicobar has the largest area of about 1405 sq.kms. Of the total islands of this territory, only about 38 are inhabited.

History

The history of A & N Islands can be found in the decennial Census Reports, Louis 1912, Bonnington 1932 and other published works like those Klauss 1903 and Whitehead 1924. The first reliable historic reference to these islands is in the writings of Chinese Buddhist monk, I' Tsing, made in 627 AD, who described these islands as "The land of the naked people". Later, mention of these islands is found in the collections of early Arab notes of the 9th century of India and China where the people of Andaman have been called "Angamainans" and the people of Nicobar have been called "Lankabalus". The ancient Arab mariners mentioned that they bartered ambergris and coconut for iron. In the earliest Hindu mythology, the "Ramayana", the Andaman islands were believed to be a land of "Hanuman". The Malayans used to refer to them as "Hanuman" and from Malaya, the knowledge of Andaman first spread to the different parts of the world.

Probably the name, Andaman, of the islands is a distorted form of "Hanuman", or "Monkey people", the aboriginal antagonist of the Arya immigrants in India. Marco Polo, who passed by these islands in 1290, on his way to China, called these Islands as " Angamanian" . He observed that the local inhabitants " are most cruel generation and eat anybody they can catch if not of their own race". Friar Ordoric, another European traveler who visited the Andamans in 1322, refers to the inhabitants of these Islands as "dog faced" and "cannibals". Nicolo Conti who came to Andamans in 1440, called these Islands as "Andamania", the Islands of gold.

East India company had consolidated its hold in southern India by the middle of 18th century and the British were interested in having a place of shelter for ships in distress during the season of monsoon. In 1777, John Ritchie reported that 'In whatever light these islands are considered, a thorough knowledge of them will appear to be of great utility. On 19th December, 1788, Lt. Archibald Blair of the Indian Navy was deputed to survey the Andamans. After his day's survey on, Lt. Blair reported that the port in South Andaman was suitable for settlement. On 12th June 1789, it was decided by the Governor General in Council to colonise these Islands. Blair sailed for the Andamans in September 1789, accompanied by some artificers, labourers and soldiers. By the 25th October 1789, Blair was able to clear some land and put up the first settlement. In August 1790, the settlers had almost cleared the sight selected by Blair in Chatham Island where they planted vegetable and fruit trees. In November 1792, it was decided to move to a new settlement in North Andaman and the same was closed in May 1796. Again, on 11th November, 1844, two ships were wrecked and 620 persons found themselves on an inhospitable island where they were constantly threatened by the tribal population. The Andaman committee was appointed to look into this matter with Dr. Frederick John Mouat as the president. They examined various sites and then selected the place where the first settlement was set up by Blair. Actually, Blair was complimented for his sense of judgment and in honor of the first surveyor, this place was named as Port Blair. On 15th January, 1845, it was decided by the Governor General in Council to establish a penal settlement on the Andamans for convicts sentenced to imprisonment and to transportation for the crime of Mutiny and rebellion and other offenses connected therewith. About the early history of the Nicobar group of Islands, very little is known. The Chola king of South India who had maritime interests came in contact with these islands. In the Great Thanjavur Inscription of 1050 AD of Chola kings, the Nicobar Islands were referred to as "Nakavaram" which means the "Land of the Naked". This was probably due to the appearance of these islanders, the body bare and a loin cloth with tail, hanging out. From 16th century onwards, there have been frequent references to these islands in the writings of voyagers. Traders from India,

Burma, Penang and the Straits settlement came to these islands chiefly for coconuts. A & N Islands, especially Car Nicobar and Nancowry, gradually flourished as important trading centers. In 1711, the first attempt was made by French Jesuits, but they were not able to withstand and soon succumbed. In 1756, the Danes took possession of these islands for colonisation and set up their headquarters in Kamorta and till 1848 repeated attempts were made by them which finally failed. In 1869, the Nicobar Islands were taken by the British with the consent of Denmark and a branch of Andaman penal settlement of 1869 was closed down in 1888 and the British were not interested in setting up an elaborate administrative structure in the Nicobar Islands due to continued expenditure, difficulties in maintaining establishment and other reasons such as malarial climate, absence of moral, social and religious restraints and loss of transportation.

With the increased tempo of freedom movement, the number of prisoners, sent to the Andamans, went on increasing. With the reforms of 1919, a general amnesty was granted to all the prisoners in the Andamans. But the rebellious outbursts in Burma and in the southern states of India kept the number of prisoners, coming into Andamans on the increase. The constitutional reforms of 1935 necessitated a thorough revision of the policy. In September 1937, the first batch of prisoners left the Andamans and by January 1938, all the prisoners were released. During the Second World War, the islands were under the Japanese occupation from March 1942 to October 1945. Again, these islands were occupied by the British. When India gained her independence in 1947, A&N Islands remained annexed with her. The A&N Islands (Protection of Aboriginal Tribals) Act was passed in 1956, under which entry into tribal areas was prohibited and no outsider could carry on trade or industry in the islands without the license of the A&N administration. Since November 1956 A&N Islands were constituted into a Union Territory of India. Though geographically these islands are far apart from the mainland (of India), they constitute a part of the Indian Union and are administered by the President of

India through Chief Commissioner upto 1983 and from 1984 onwards through Lt. Governor whose Headquarter is at Port Blair.

Other Features

The spread of A&N Islands shows that these islands were once connected with the Arkan Yoma of Burma in the north and with the Indonesian islands in the south. In the Andamans the important rock formations are of sedimentary origin and are known as the Port Blair series and the Archipelago series. The Port Blair series consists of non-calcareous gray sandstones and embedded shells with occasional pockets of poor coal and pale gray limestones. The former is older than the later. In Long Island, cream colored porous limestones and calcareous sandstones are found in large quantity. In Interview Island the principal rock formations are limestones. In Little Andaman the predominant rock formations are limestones of various types.

The Nicobar Islands form part of the outer non-volcanic islands which extend from Sumatra to Arkan. The rocks of this territory are of recent age and white porous coral and shale limestones cover the greater part of the Car Nicobar Islands. Nancowry, Kamorta and other parts of the Nicobar group contains sandstones. The hills of Katchal are composed of calcareous sandstones and marble slate. In Little Nicobar and Great Nicobar the principle rocks are micaceous and soft micaceous.

Topographically, the Andaman Islands are, generally, hilly and are characterised by low range of hills and narrow valleys, except coastal stretches. The places, in which the hills go down, indicate that the islands are part of the submerged mountains . The land in the Andamans often sheer off the sea, clearly suggesting to their being the visible ridges and summits of sunken ranges. The ranges are form north to south but several spurs and ridges run off the main ranges in all directions indicating a very confused topography.

Generally speaking, the hills on the eastern side of the islands are somewhat higher than those on the west, the highest point in all the areas being "Saddle Peak" which is in the North Andaman Island. The height of Saddle Peak is 2400 feet (800 mtrs.) above the mean sea level. The slopes are moderate to steep, ragged and liable to suffer from erosion. Flat lands are comparatively scarce and confined to some of the larger valleys as in Betapur and Diglipur. Except for Little Andaman, Interview Islands which are more or less flat, the other islands in the Andaman group have little flat land. The islands in the Nicobar group are largely flat and gently undulating and surrounded by coral reefs and shallow seas of width varying from a few yards to a mile or more. The Nicobar group of islands has narrow but stretches off sandy beaches. Generally, they include more of easy ground. Car Nicobar and Katchal Island of Nicobar group are almost flat and others include hilly terrain. The highest elevation here in Nicobar group is less than 700 meters. In Little Nicobar and Great Nicobar the land surface is very irregular, often broken by steep hill ranges and valleys of varying width with more or less perennial streams flowing therein.

The climate of A&N Islands can be described as tropical and warm. But this is tempered by pleasant sea breeze. As far as the humidity is concerned, it is very high for the most part of the year. The Islands have been exposed to both the monsoons and experience north westerly winds from November to December and south easterly gale from May to October. The weather is normally smooth from January to the middle of February and to a less extent in October. From February to May is the hot season and April is the hottest month. From the point of viewof comparison, the climate of the Nicobar islands is different because of the difference between the rainy and the dry season in the Nicobar group. However, there is not much variation in the climatic conditions of the two groups of Islands.

In the Andaman group of Islands, the soils are generally fertile, supporting a varied type of forest vegetation, sandy alluvial soil, resulting from the deposition of fine material from the higher slopes in saline swamps and creeks, support mangrove forests that fringe the islands in the sheltered coasts and Island creeks. The richer gray, brown and red soils, derived from the sandstones and serpentine rocks, support the major crops especially the forest crops. The soils of A&N Islands vary from heavy clay to clay loams, gravely loams and sandy loams, the former being found mostly in the valley areas. Soil depth differs from the slopes and the shallow soils characterise the higher elevations. The soils have low moisture retention capacity. Humus or organic matter is comparatively lacking even in the forest soils, having been washed away by the heavy rainfall assisted by the steep slopes and the loose texture of the soils. In the Nicobar group of Islands, the coralline alluvium on the high beaches is so common, along their coast. This supports rich forest or tree vegetation. The soil set up of Nicobar is eminently suitable for coconut cultivation. In the flat lands and along the river and stream banks, the soil is fresh water alluvium. Where conditions tend to be swampy the soil is very deep but where it is well drained, the soil is rich and fertile and supports excellent forest crops. Soils from calcareous, sand-stones are deep and fertile with luxuriant growth of forests. The hill soil tends to be shallow and rather infertile.

WATER RESOURCES

Surface Water

In any region, surface water resources (rivers, lakes) form the major sources of water for drinking, agricultural and industrial uses as well as for household needs. Since the individual islands of this territory are small in area, there is no possibility of presence of major rivers. So, only a few streams of a few kilometers in length are seen in the islands. The streams are locally called as 'nallahs', meaning streams or small rivers. A&N Islands receive, on an average, an annual rainfall of a little more than 300mm. The precipitation received from both the south west and north east monsoon is spread over a period of six to eight months. Besides the rainfall, the other sources of water are the surface water and ground water which are the direct result of the rainfall received by the area itself. In the Andaman district, the important streams are (a) Kalpong nallah (river) in North Andaman; (b) Vasundhra nallah; (c) Wrightmyo nallah; (d) Dhania nallah and (e) Sona nallah in South Andaman; (f) Rangat nallah; (g) Badam nallah; (h) Thoratang nallah; (i) Picture nallah; (j) CFO nallah; (k) Korang nallah and (1) Panchavadi nallah in Middle Andaman. In the Nicobar district, the streams are visible only in Great Nicobar Island. The important streams are (a) Galathia river; (b) Alexandria river; (c) Dongmar river; (d) Amril Kaur river; (e) Jubilee river (small) and (f) Millan river (small). In Car Nicobar there is no nallah. There is no lake or tank in these islands, except the Thilthamman tank which is situated in the heart of the Port Blair city. The important characterstics of most of these streams (nallahs) are that they are short in length and swift in flow towards east or west, resulting in a quick run off into the sea. During the rainy season, the (nallahs) streams are full of water and scarcity of water occurs only for four months. Even in the rainy season, scarcity of water for industrial activities is there in almost all the islands since there is no dam in these islands except one named Dhanikari dam in Port Blair.

As far as Port Blair, the only urban centre in the islands having a population of around 50,000, is concerned the drinking water is being supplied from Dhanikari dam which was constructed in, and has been supplying potable water since the end of 1973. This dam's storage capacity is 900 million gallons and is capable of supplying 1.5 million gallons of water per day to the Port Blair city. Thiltamman tank, near God Vetrimalai Murugan Temple, was supplying drinking water to Port Blair city. But after the construction of the Dhanikari dam the tank is not utilised as a source of drinking water. It also reserves a considerable amount of water throughout the year, and there is no other major storage of fresh water in the islands.

Ground Water Resources

The geography of A&N Islands is such that there are difficulties in the development of ground water resources. Saline aquifers (the interior rock zones having water) are encountered at shallow depths. The Central Ground Water Board (CGWB) has undertaken systematic hydrological surveys, and 11 promising sites bearing fresh water were pin-pointed in the South Andaman Islands. The surveys have revealed that shallow dug wells in the sandstones of South Andaman are capable of yielding 300 to 400 cu.m. per day. Sparings, emanating from the sandstones and volcanic rocks also have an average yield of 10 to 15 litres per minute during the lean season. In some places CGWB has succeeded in drilling tube wells. The well, dug in the God Alaikaddal Ayyanar campus with medium depth, gives very good drinking water. People of the surrounding areas take water from the well. In order to provide water to the whole population of these islands, it is essential to have conjuncture use of surface and ground water resources.

A&N Islands abound in forest wealth. The forests are the main source of the territory's revenue and the major basis of its economy. The only industry worth the name found there is wood based industry. The forests provide adequate variety and quantity of trees. Some high quality hardwood trees, which are scarce or not seen in the mainland, are found in these islands in abundance. The Padauk trees, whose value as raw material for furniture is invaluable, are common in these islands. The forest area of this territory is 7,171 sq.kms. which is about 86% of the total land area of A&N Islands. It is to be appreciated that whereas India as a whole has only 22.9% of its geographical area under forests, A&N Islands has nearly four times that of the national average (86.41%). This comprises 3,059 sq.kms. of reserve forests and 17 sq.kms. of protected forests and 4,112 sq.kms. for proposed reserve forests.

The forests of A&N Islands are unique in character and possess enormous biological diversity. Of the 2,200 rare species of trees found in A&N Islands, about 200 species (10%) are endemic to these islands, but are found in Malaysia, Burma, Indonesia and Polynesian islands. Floristically, the forests have been classified by Champin and Seth into the following groups :

- Tidal Swamp Forests (mangrove forests)
- Littoral Forests
- Andaman Moist Deciduous Forests
- Andaman semi Evergreen Forests
- Bamboo Brakes
- Cane Brakes
- Southern Hilltop Tropical Evergreen Forests
- Andaman Tropical Evergreen Forests and
- Giant Evergreen Forests

The distribution and extent of each type of forest depends primarily on the climatic and topographic factors. The Forest Department has made an assessment of the wood potential of these islands. It is estimated that about 3.63 lakhs cu.m. of different varieties of wood which includes 1,67,000 cu.m. of wood for plywood, 1,21,000 cu.m. of hardwood and 75,000 cu.m. of softwood will be available on a sustained basis.

PLANTATION RESOURCES

Plantation resources of A&N islands include coconut, arecanut, rubber, red oil palm and other plantations like cashew nut, nutmeg, cinnamon etc., which are discussed below.

Coconut

The location of these islands in the tropical belt and the high amount of rainfall provide favourable conditions for the natural growth of coconut plants. The area under coconut cultivation in these islands is about 22,000 hectares with a production of about 7.3 crore of nuts per annum. The plantations are owned either by individuals or by co-operatives and are mostly concentrated in the islands of the Nicobar district. Despite heavy consumption of coconut by the Nicobarese, the bulk of the production is sent to the mainland. Nearly 2,020 hectares of A&N Islands are under arecanut plantation with a production of about 3,030 tons per annum. Arecanut is grown both in the Andaman as well as in the Nicobars. The Nicobar Group of Islands accounts for the bulk of the areas as well as the production. Arecanut is mainly sent to the mainland.

Rubber

The Rubber Board made an assessment in the year 1959 that about 4000 hectares in Katchal, 1200 hecatres in Ruthland and about 2400 hectares in Great Nicobar, could be brought under rubber plantation. The soil as well as the agro-climatic conditions in the territory, particularly in the Nicobar Group of Islands, are suitable for the introduction of rubber plantation on a large scale. At present, rubber plantation has been taken up in the South Andaman Group of islands and Katchal islands of the Nicobar Group of Islands. In South Andaman, plantations were raised on revenue lands whereas in Katchal Island, the forest lands were utilised for this purpose. So far, an area of 614 hectares has been covered, out of which 593 hectares belongs to the Rubber Board. Latex, a product from the rubber plantations is tapped. It is converted into rubber sheets and the entire production is sent to the mainland.

Red Oil Palm

The Forest Department initiated, on an experimental basis, red oil palm cultivation in Little Andaman in 1975 and covered an area of 2,400 hectares. The area was, however, restricted to 200 hectares only under instructions from the Government of

India pending study with regard to the effect of red oil palm plantations on the environment and ecology of these islands. The experiment was subsequently taken over by the Forest Plantation Development Corporation Ltd., which started functioning from 1st April, 1977. About 1600 hectares of area has been planted so far. The red oil palm plantation involves clear felling of the rain forests.

Other plantations

The other plantation crops like pepper, cloves, nutmeg, cashew nut, cinnamon etc., are being tried on an experimental basis in South Andaman. Pepper, cloves and cashew nuts are showing encouraging results.

MINERAL RESOURCES

In A&N Islands, the mineral resources are very limited. Chromium, copper, iron, silver, coal, limestone, oil and gas are the mineral resources found in the Islands. But no important deposit of any mineral has been found. Exploratory activities of the ONGC in A&N Islands were conducted in 1959 when geological surveys were started in the on-land area, followed by geophysical surveys in the off-shore areas. The first exploratory well AN-1, located in diligent Strait area, was drilled in 1980, and gas was extracted. Three more wells, drilled on the same geological structure, proved dry. Two more prospects (AN-2-1) in the western off-shore and AN-3-1 to the east of Ritchies Archipelago were also drilled. Thus a total of six wells were drilled in three prospects. At present, one is operating in the Andaman off-shore area. As per the Planning Commission, 1986 projected production of gas in Andaman & Nicobar Islands was 70 MMT in 1985-90 and 2230 to 4310 MMT in 1990-2000, where the projected production of oil is 1.22 to 1.45 MMT in 1990-2000.

LIVESTOCK RESOURCES

The livestock of these islands consist mainly of cattle

buffaloes, goats, poultry and pigs. Initially, all the livestock farming except rearing of pigs was undertaken to meet the requirements of the human population of these islands. Only very recently rearing of goats, buffaloes and poultry was started.

MARINE RESOURCES

The deep sea around A&N Islands, the numerous inlets, bays and creeks are the abode of marine resources. With the declaration of 200 miles beyond the coast-line as our Economic zone, A&N Islands has a vast area around it for exploitation of the untapped marine resources. On the western side, the entire 200 miles' extent can be exploited. On the other three sides, A&N Islands has to equally share the sea space with the neighbouring countries. Various assessments were made in the past by the Indian experts on the availability of marine resources in the seas, surrounding the A&N Islands, but no systematic study has so far been made to know the actual quantum of resources available for utilisation. On this basis, the total net weight of the resources available is estimated to be about 1.07 million tonnes. The marine resources of A&N Islands may broadly be divided into two groups as fish and shell.

Fish

It has been estimated that an area of 1,19,600 Sq. miles around these islands has potential for fishing. The assessed fishery resources in this area is between 5 to 10 lakhs tonnes of fish per annum. But it is reported that the present catch in these islands is only 9692 tonnes. This clearly indicates that there exists a vast scope for the development, exploitation and utilisation of the fish resources of these islands. Sardines and mackerals, the two important varieties of fish, are found towards the shore and can be exploited by the small boats using pursesuines and other nets. The entire region is full of sharks. The rocky bottom has great potential for percoid fishes (porches). According to a survey of marine resources, conducted very recently by the Government of India Exploratory Fisheries Project and the Fisheries Department, it has come to light that a large number of varieties of fish having commercial value are available.

Three important species of the Tuna are found in the waters of A&N Islands. They are 1. Skip jack (Katusuwpnus pelamis); 2. Yellow fin (Tbunnus neothunnus) (Albaesies macrpierus); 3. Big eye (Thunnus parathunnus) (Obsus mebachi). A stock of 25,000 tonnes of Yellow fin and Big eye in the sea around A&N Islands has been estimated. About 50,000 tonnes of Skip jack is also postulated for A&N Islands. An item of commercial importance, found in plenty in the shallow waters around the main Islands, is the Seaslug or Beach-de-mer (Holothurian). Out of nearly 40 species available, six species are of high commercial value which could yield substantial foreign exchange. About a dozen species of prawns are also found in these waters.

Shell

A&N Islands is on abode of innumerable species of shells of various shapes and colours. Some of them have very high commercial value and many others form excellent show pieces. Turbo and Troches, the two species having high commercial value, are collected in plenty and are sent/exported to the mainland. The shells are used as raw materials in the Shell Handicraft Industrial Units which is a growing sector. The fancy articles like necklace, bracelets, lamp shades and other ornaments are manufactured by the units. These items attract both domestic and foreign tourists. Besides theshells, Five finger Chanks, Sacred Chanks, Pearly Oysters, Mussels, Clams, Cowries and numerous other varieties of high value and gastropod shells are found all along the shores. Their flesh is generally tasty and some are delicious. One more evidence to show the abundance of the marine resources is the apprehension of the foreign vessels by the Coast Guard, Navy and Police Department when they entered the coastal area of A&N Islands for fishing.

LAND RESOURCES

The total land area of A&N Islands is 8293 sq.kms. out of which the Andaman Group of Islands covers an area of 6340 sq.kms. and the Nicobar Group of Islands the remaining 1953 sq.kms. The available land resources of any country exercise a lasting effect on the economic life of man or nation because the production of raw materials depends greatly on the nature of landscapes. In the hilly tracts, agriculture and industry generally cannot flourish. The result is that the production of wealth in these tracts is less and therefore, only a sparse population can be supported. In Andaman islands, the available land resources are being utilised.

ECONOMY

The economy of A&N Islands consists of agriculture, trade, commerce and industry. At present, very little quantity of paddy, sugarcane, banana, sweet potato, papaya, rabi pulse and vegetables are cultivated. Among the Andaman cash crops namely cashewnut, coconut, arecanut are grown. The last two are actively cultivated but the cashewnut is not taken seriously by the people of Andamans. Some other vegetables like tomato, potato, cabbage, onion, cauliflower, beans, carrot, green chillies etc., are brought from the mainland. As far as the trade and commerce is concerned, all types of trade are dominated by the Tamilians and Panjabis. But they purchase things from the mainland only. However, the inter-islands traders purchase goods from the Port Blair's traders only. Though the wholesale and retail trade are common, the special type of trade namely "Govt. Order Supply" is very famous in these islands. As far as the industry is concerned, all types of industries are found in A&N Islands. But majority of the industrial units are based on wood. They satisfy the tourists with their handicrafts. Major portion of the cash inflow is from the budget allocation by the Central Government. The status of the economy is not even developing but is at its infant stage with the full scope of growth and development. Tourism and industry are the only possible sectors in this territory which can develop the economy of the A&N Islands.

ADMINISTRATIVE SET-UP

A&N Islands, being a Union Territory, are under the direct rule of the President of India through the Lt. Governor as the Administrator, who is assisted by the Chief Secretary, Secretary (Planning)-cum-Development Commissioner, Finance Secretary-cum- Chief Pay and Accounts Officer, Judicial Secretary, Secretary Shipping and Transport and Secretary to Lt. Governor. The A&N Administration continues to conduct its business in 19 major departments, namely, Forest, Police, Public Works Marine, Civil Supply, Transport, Agriculture, Animal Husbandry, Fisheries, Co-operatives, Industries, Education, Medical & Public Health, Revenue, Justice, Electricity, Labour, Rehabilitation and Pay & Accounts .

Besides this, there are also a number of Central Government Departments such as Andaman Harbour Works, Field Publicity unit of the Ministry of Information and Broadcasting, Anthropological Survey of India, Lighthouses and Lightships Department, P&T Department, Zoological Survey of India, Botanical Survey of India, Meteorological Department, etc. in A&N Islands. Principal Chief Conservator of Forest and the Chief Engineer, APWD, are functioning as ex-officio Secretaries to the Administration. Pradesh Council was constituted for A&N Islands on June 20, 1981, on the pattern of the erstwhile Arunachal Pradesh Council, having functions of advisory nature. The council consists of an Administrator and 29 members.

3

POPULATION OF ANDAMAN AND NICOBAR ISLANDS

The development of a particular state, place or a destination fully depends on the people who live there. As quality of water determines the quality of healthy life, the activity of the people determines the quality and quantity of the development of the place. All economic activities must, necessarily, be carried out by the people of the state for better overall development. Tourism industry is a newly born infant, requiring a lot of vitaminised economic activities. To study the nature, possibilities of growth, prospects, etc., of the tourism activity of a particular destination, it is important to know and visualize the characteristics of the population. Major portion of the total tourism attractions consist of social, economic and cultural activities including the fairs and festivals which are inherited. Tourists are like growing children. They are very much interested in discovering the new things. They are attracted by different activities of the people from different places. Dresses, the way of dressing, likes and dislikes , eating habits, ideas, adaptability, acceptability, hospitality etc., differ from people to people. In A & N islands people from different regions, religions, faiths etc., live in harmony with one another. It is the mini India.

Population

As per the 1991 census, 38 islands of this territory were found to be inhabited. These islands include Ross Island which is completely under the occupation of the Defence Authorities and Chatham Islands which is connected by a bridge with Port Blair but is not treated as a part of Port Blair. Out of the 38 islands, 25 islands are located in Andaman district and 13 in the Nicobar district. Except Nicobarese and primitive tribals, the rest are the people from the mainland - refugees from former East Pakistan (now Bangladesh), repatriates from Sri Lanka and Burma, resettled Ex-servicemen and descendents of the prisoners held at Port Blair. There is another set of population (migrants) from Tamil Nadu, Andhra Pradesh, Kearla and Bihar (particularly from Ranchi) who are labourers. The population of these islands is a heterogenous one, with a mixture of diverse communities from the mainland. So A&N Island is a miniature India. People of all the states in India live in these Islands in harmony with their own culture. The population of A&N Islands is discussed under the following sub-heads.

(a) Groups of Population
(b Growth of Population
(c) Density
(d) Sex Ratio
(e Literacy
(f) Language and religion, and
(g) Working population

Groups of Population

As already mentioned, in A&N islands people from different regions, religions, races, faiths etc., continue to live together in a peaceful manner. Some were invited to these islands and some came to these islands on employment and some started economic activities relating to trade, commerce and industry. So the population of these islands can be broadly divided into four groups. They are 1) Tribals, 2) Andaman Indians, 3) New Settlers and 4) Government employees from the mainland.

Tribals

The aboriginals or the tribals of these islands are the original inhabitants. The total number of the tribal population as per 1991 census was 26770 which is 9.5% of the total population of A&N islands. The tribal population and its decadal growth are given in Table 3.1 and Table 3.2 respectively.

Table 3.1
Tribal Population of A & N Isands

Tribals	1951	1961	1971	1981	1991
Andaman Islands					
Andamanese	23	19	24	26	NA
Onges	150*	129	112	97	NA
Jarawas	50*	500*	NE	NE	NA
Sentinalese	-	50*	NE	NE	NA
Nicobar Islands					
Nicobarese	11902	13903	17874	21984	NA
Shompens	20*	71	92	223	NA
A&N Islands	12145	14672	18102	22361	26770

Source : Census Department, Basic Statistics, A&N Administration, Port Blair.
NE - Not Enumerated, NA - Not Available, * - Estimated

Table 3.2
Growth Rate of Tribal Population of A&N Islands

Year	Population	Growth Rate	% to the total Population
1951	12145	-	39.2
1961	14672	20.8	23.1
1971	18102	23.4	15.7
1981	22361	23.5	11.9
1991	26770	19.7	9.5

Source : Compiled from previous Table.

ANDAMAN TRIBALS

The aboriginals or the tribals of the Andaman Islands are

known as Andaman Tribals. They are of Negrito stock/race. Their main occupation is food gathering. Andaman tribals are of four types namely:

1. Jarawas
2. Sentinalese
3. Onges and
4. Great Andamanese

Jarawas

Among the four tribals, Jarawas are forest dwellers and hostile. They inhabit and live in the west coast of South and Middle Andamans in the reserved forest area. They are claimed to be one of the purest and most primitive races in the world with a human memory "who live on hunting and food gathering". The jarawas do not have any relation with the other types of tribals and non-tribals and that's why nothing is known about their life style and economy, habits and characteristics. They look dark like other Negrito tribes and have thick skin and long but curly hair. Both the males and females are tall. It is understood that they love deers and like red colour. They do not wear dresses of any type. But they wear necklace, big mala waist bands, head bands made out of sea-shells, palm leaves and some bones. Sometimes they decorate their body with clay. They collect fruit honey, tuber from different plants, fish monitor lizard, wild pig etc., for their food. But there is no evidence that they have killed deer and birds who are very friendly with Jarawas. Till 1973, the Jarawas could not be contacted. In 1974, the A & N Administration, with the joint efforts of Anthropology Department, successfully contacted one group of Jarawas and presented them gifts. From 1974 onwards, at irregular intervals, the A&N Administration has been contacting the Jarawas and presenting them gifts, in the form of coconuts, red coloured clothes, drinking water, other eatables etc., No attempt, however, has been made to stay with them because the behaviour of the Jarawas is still unpredictable.

Sentinalese

The Sentinalese are also forest dwellers and are very hostile. They are unapproachable. They inhabit and live in the isolated island named North Sentinal Island, situated in the west direction to the Port Blair. The Sentinalese are left alone in the reserved small island, the area of which is about 50 sq.kms. During the years 1967, 1978, 1982, 1984 – 1989, frequent attempts have been made to contact them by the Anthropoligical department. But the last one was fairly successful in which the Sentinalese felt free to come close to the venturers' boat in their (Sentinalese) canoes to pick up the gifts of coconuts which were floated by the venturers in the sea. The Sentinalese live in small sized huts under the trees They use arrow and bow, plucking stick, arrow cum spear, bamboo pot, nautilus shells, fishing net, cane basket, waist band, grinding stone, hammer stone, resin, pig skull, dug out canoe, multi-pronged wooden harpoon spear etc., to serve their different ends.

Onges

Onges are a friendly tribe among the four Negrito tribes. They inhabit and live in the Little Andaman Islands and come in contact with outside civilisation, following the setting up of the settlement. They are very friendly with the non tribals. Occasionally, they come out of their residence or islands. "They are of dark colour, short statured with unusual growth of buttocks (both males and females). Their hands and feet are small but strong. Their eyes are bright and clear white in contrast to their complexion. Their teeth are remarkably strong and are retained till old age though not regularly cleaned". Most of the Onges are very weak and some of them suffer from a disease like tuberculosis. Now the A & N Administration has opened a dispensary and individual health cards are being maintained. The local administration has constructed some modern double storeyed residential houses for them. They call themselves "Onges" a verbal noun meaning of "Man Being".

Great Andamanese

Great Andamanese are also one of the Andaman tribes like Negrito race. Once they dominated the full South Andaman Islands with an estimated population of 5000 but due to the ill-treatment by the authorities in different years their strength has come down to 26 as per 1981 census. The main reason for this is that they have been contacted by the non tribals. "Great Andamanese were enjoying a free, independent and healthy life, free from disease. But the contact with the outside world brought epidemics like cholera, small pox, measles and contagious diseases like T.B, V.D etc.". Great Andamanese are short in height. The colour of their skin is light black. Now-a-days they have started wearing all types of dresses including 'T' shirts, available in the market.

NICOBAR TRIBALS

The aboriginals or the tribals of the Nicobar Islands are known as Nicobar Tribals. They are completely different from Andaman Tribals. Their main occupation is also food gathering. Nicobar Tribals are of two types namely, Nicobaries and Shompens.

Nicobarese

Among the tribal population of A & N islands, the Nicobarese are the advanced and most civilised and developing tribe. They wear good dresses and use cosmetics to be at par with the non tribals They love one another and non tribals as well. Now-a-days, they get on employment in almost all the governement jobs. They are very free and frank without any cunningness like others. Even they have started marrying the non tribals particularly mainlanders. They inhabit and live almost in all the parts of Nicobar group of islands. Nicobarese are also known as Holchu, living in fairly well organised communities. According to 1981 census their population was 21,727. Most of the Nicobarese are living in Car Nicobar and to a less extent in Nancowry and Katchal. Estimated and actual population is given in the Table 3.1. Their population nearly doubled in 80 years (1901– 1981). On the basis of locality they live in, the Nicobarese can be divided into six tribes as given below:

Name	Locality
1. Car Nicobarese	Car Nicobar
2. Chowrite (Chowre Nicobarese)	Chowra
3. Teressan (Terrese Nicobarese)	Teressa and Bompokka
4. South Nicobarese	Pilowmillow Little Nicobar etc.
5. Central Nicobarese	Nancowry, Kamorta, Trinket, and Katchal
6. Shompens	Interior places of Great Nicobar

Shompens

Another type of primitive tribes of Nicobar tribals is the Shompens. They inhabit the Great Nicobar Island. They are not like Jarawas, Sentinalese, Onges or Great Andamanese who belong to Negrito race. But Shompens are from Mongoloid race. They live in interior jungles and feel very shy to come infront of any human being who is not of their race. They eat coconuts, bananas, pandanus, tubers, fish, wild pig, lizards etc. The Shompens do have some business relations with the Nicobarese. With the help of Yatrik (a department of Govt. of India) the local administration has constructed some infrastructural facilities and helps the Shompens to lead a peaceful life. A&N Administration has opened a school in their area to give formal and informal education. As per the records, their population is increasing.

ANDAMAN INDIANS

The Andaman Indians are the people of the mainland who have settled in the islands mainly in South Andaman under unusual circumstances. When A&N Islands were under penal settlement, i.e., during 1858-1945, the entire population of A&N Islands except the tribals or aboriginals consisted of convicts, administrative personnel concerned with the convicts, merchants, etc. The convicts formed the major portion of the population. The penal settlement was abolished in the year 1945 by remitting all sentences and offering repatriation. The population in 1947 was 14,000. The local born were recorded as Andaman Indians in the 1951 census. The estimated population of the local born in 1987 was about 40,000 and they were descendants of the convicts. A&N Gazetteer of 1908 describes the local born as descendants of the convicts born in the settlement and the permanent resident there. Bonnington (1931:19) described local population or community as descendants from Indian convicts' parents on both sides who had settled in Andamans. They have been characterised by strong unity among themselves and also constitute and an amalgamated society.

NEW SETTLERS

The New Settlers include colonisers who are mainly refugees from East Bengal, Bihar and Kerala. They settled permanently on cleared forest land which is suitable for agriculture and pastoral occupations. At present the settlers do the business in various forms like cultivation, producing vegetables, work in factories, business, mines and quarries, etc. Some settlers have constructed good houses and let out some of these for rent. By and large, the settlers lead a very happy life in these islands.

GOVERNMENT EMPLOYEES

This group of population includes persons who have come over to these islands from the mainland on government employment, transfer, deputation, etc. This group includes employees of A&N administration ranging from secretaries to clerks, all teachers and employees of the schools, colleges, institutes and institutions, employees of Banks, Public Works

Department, all departments of A & N Administration, Govt. of India, Defence, Telecommunications, Census, Anthropological Survey of India, Botanical Survey of India, Zoological Survey of India, etc.

GROWTH OF POPULATION

Growth Rate

The total population of A&N Islands as per 1991 census was 2,80,661 constituting 1,54,346 males and 1,26,292 females. It formed only 0.03% of the total population of the country as a whole. The territory of A&N Islands was placed at 29th position by the size of population at the 1991 census. Table 3.3 indicates the changes in the population of A&N Islands since 1901.

Table 3.3
Population of A&N Islands since 1901 (in No.)

Census Year	Andamans	Nicobars	Total	Percentage of decadal variation
1901	18138	6511	24649	–
1911	17641	8818	26459	(+) 7.34
1921	17814	9272	27086	(+) 2.37
1931	19223	10240	29463	(+) 8.78
1941	21316	12452	33768	(+) 14.61
1951	18962	12009	30971	(-) 8.28
1961	48985	14563	63548	(+) 105.19
1971	93468	21665	115133	(+) 81.17
1981	158287	30454	188741	(+) 63.93
1991	241453	39208	280661	(+) 48.70

Source : Census Report 1991, A&N Islands.

There was a steady and slow growth of population from 1911 to 1941 , but there was a sudden decrease in population in the decade 1941-51 both in the Andaman district and in the Nicobar district . The reason for the sudden decrease might be due to the second world war. Table 3.4 shows the growth rate of population in A&N Islands from 1901.

Table 3.4
Growth Rate of Population in A & N Islands
Percentage decadal variation in population

Decade	A&N Islands	Andamans District	Nicobars District
1901-11	(+) 7.34	(-) 2.74	(+) 35.43
1911-21	(+) 2.37	(+) 0.98	(+) 5.50
1921-31	(+) 8.78	(+) 7.91	(+) 10.44
1931-41	(+) 14.61	(+) 10.89	(+) 21.60
1941-51	(-) 8.28	(-) 11.04	(-) 3.56
1951-61	(+) 105.19	(+) 158.33	(+) 21.27
1961-71	(+) 81.17	(-) 90.81	(+) 48.77
1971-81	(+) 63.93	(-) 69.35	(+) 40.57
1981-91	(+) 48.70	(+) 52.54	(+) 28.74

Source : Basic Statistics & Census Report 1991, Census Department, Port Blair.

A remarkable decennial growth rate of 93% was recorded during the decade 1971-81 for A&N Islands as against the growth rate of 24.75% registerred for the country as a whole . But during the next decadal year 1981-91, its growth rate was 48.7% in A&N Island as against the growth rate of 23% registered for the country as a whole. The districts of A&N Islands recorded a growth rate of 52.54% and 28.74 % respectively , during the decade 1981-91. The population of the entire territory which was 115133 in the year 1971 increased to 2,80,661 in the year 1991, an increase of over 140% in two decades which was much higher than the All India bi-decadal growth rate of 54% . This spurt in population which was much higher than the normal growth rate was due to large scale influx of people into A&N Islands in search of employment opportunities, induction of families for settlement under various rehabilitation programmes and increase in the strength of defence personnel stationed here. There are seven tehsils in this territory, of which five are in the Andaman Islands and two in the Nicobar Islands. For the information of the tourists, the tehsilwise, islandwise population in A&N islands is given in Table 3.5.

Table 3.5
Tehsilwise, Islandwise Population

District/ Island/ Tehsil/ Town	Population (in No.)
Andaman & Nicobar Islands	**2,80,661**
Andaman District	**2,41,453**
Diglipur Tehsil	23,734
1. Narcondam Island	17
2. East Island	29
3. North Andaman Island (Part)	23,396
4. Smith Island	292
Mayabunder Tehsil	21,570
North Andaman Island (Part)	8,092
5. Stewart Island	2
6. Curlew Island	2
7. Aves Island	3
8. Interview Island	19
9. Middle Andaman Island (Part)	13,452
Rangat Tehsil	33,368
Middle Andaman Island (Part)	31,449
10. Prolob Island	2
11. Long Island	1,917
Port Blair Tehsil	1,23,504
12. North Passage Island	47
13. Strait Island	33
14. Baratang Island	5,560
15. Peel Island	4
16. Havelock Island	3,681
17. John Lawrance Island	53
18. Neil Island	2,463
19. South Andaman Island (Part)	98,828
20. Rutland Island	562
21. North Sentinel Island	26
22. Little Andaman Island	12,247
Ferrargunj Tehsil	39,277
South Andaman Island (Part)	39,268
23. Flat Bay Island	2
24. Viper Island	7
Nicobars District	39,208

Contd...

Car Nicobar Tehsil	19,336
1. Car Nicobar Island	19,336
Nancowry Tehsil	19,872
2. Chowra Island	1,225
3. Teressa Island	1,779
4. Bampoka Island	51
5. Katchal Island	5,072
6. Nancowry Island	1,014
7. Kamorta Island	2,973
8. Trinket Island	350
9. Pulomilo Island	122
10. Little Nicobar Island	308
11. Kondul Island	147
12. Great Nicobar	6,831

Source: Census Report, 1991, Census Department, Port Blair - Basic Statistics.

Table 3. 6
Tehsil-wise Density of Population

Sl.No. Tehsil	No. of Persons per sq.kms			
	1961	1971	1981	1991
1. Diglipur	5	11	18	27
2. Mayabunder	4	6	10	16
3. Rangat	7	14	23	31
4. Port Blair & Ferrargunj	10	20	33	52
5. Car Nicobar	77	105	120	152
6. Nancowry	3	4	8	12
A & N Islands	8	14	23	34

Source : Census Report 1991 & Basic Statistics, A&N Administration.

The population density, as per above tables, of A & N Islands as a whole has been increasing but at a moderate rate. During 1981 and 1991 the density suddenly increased from 14 persons per sq.km to 23 persons and from 23 to 34 in the respective decadal years. The main reason for this is the improved infrastructural facilities developed in these islands. As per the Table 3.6 the Car Nicobar tehsil is thickly populated because the Nicobar tribals do not want to come out of their islands. Among the other tehsils, Port Blair and Ferrargunj tehsils have more density that is 52 persons per sq.km. When compared with other tehsils, this density is quite high because all facilities are available only in these tehsils.

Literacy

As per 1981 census, the literacy rate in this territory was 60.25% as compared to the all India average literacy rate of 36.23%. In the year 1991, the literacy rate of A & N Islands was 73.02% as compared to the all India average literacy rate of 52.11%, a considerable increase indeed. The relatively high percentage of literacy of the total population of these islands may be due to the increase in number of educational institutions in A & N Islands. These islands have a total of about 350 educational institutions, including two Government degree colleges, one B.Ed degree college at Port Blair, and two government polytechnic institutions at Dollygunj village. The entire human resources of the islands are spread over the inhabited islands.

Language and Religion

In A & N islands the main religions are Hinduism, Islam, Christianity, Sikhism, Buddhism and Jainism. The Table 3. 7 shows the religionwise population of the islands. As per 1981 census, the Hindu population was 1,21,793 as against 70,134 in 1971 constituting 64.53% and 60.92% of the total population respectively in the respective years. This increased to 189,521 in the census year 1991 by showing an increase of 55.6% over the previous decadal year and constituting 67.5% of the total population. There was a considerable increase in the Muslim population in 1991 i.e. from 16188 in 1981 to 21354 in 1991 constituting only 7.6% of the total population. But the Christian population increased to 39.2% over the previous decadel year 1981 by consituting about 30.0% of the total population. The table also shows that the

Hindus are dominating in the A & N Islands. Next to the Hindus, come the Christians and the Muslims.

Table 3. 7
Religionwise Population of A & N islands (in No.)

Sl.No.	Religion	Population in Census year				
		1951	1961	1971	1981	1991
1.	Hindus	9294	32781	70134	121793	189521
2.	Christians	9494	17973	30342	48274	67211
3.	Muslims	4783	7398	11655	16188	21354
4.	Sikhs	126	241	865	991	1350
5.	Buddhists	1604	1707	103	127	322
6.	Jains	01	03	14	11	17
7.	Others	5669	3445	2020	1357	886
	Total	30971	63548	115133	188741	280661

Source : Census Report 1991 & Basic Statistics, A&N Administration.

As far as the languages are concerned, about 33 languages are being spoken in these islands. Of these, Tamil, Bengali, Hindi, Malayalam,Telugu, Urdu,Nicobari and Kurgu are the important languages. However, the official language in these islands, is Hindi along with English.

Working Population

The working population of A&N islands, for the purpose of this present work, is divided under five headings namely :

1. Cultivation and Agriculture
2. Industry
3. Livestock
4. Trade and Commerce
5. Government and Other Services

Cultivation includes all working population engaged in

cultivation, forestry, agriculture, farming, plantation, fishing and other allied activities. Industry includes all working population in manufacturing, processing, servicing, repairs and construction, mining and quarrying, etc. The working population concerning livestock includes all workers who engage in the rearing of livestock namely cows,goats, buffaloes, poultry, pigs, etc. Workers in trade and commerce include those engaged in trade activities, banking, transport, storage, communication, tourism, insurance, etc. The workers in Government and other services comprise people engaged in Government departments, doctors, teachers, engineers, musicians, social workers, domestic servants, etc. Table 3.8 shows the working and non working population in A&N Islands.

According to the Census year 1991, the working population was 98,901 consisting of 82,317 males and 16, 584 females, It formed 35.24% of the total population. Male working population shared 53.33% of the total male population whereas the female working population formed only 13.13% of the total female population. Regarding the employment pattern, 19.7% of the work force was engaged in cultivation, 11.5% in livestock activities, 23.5% in industries, 13.6% in trade and commerce and 31.7% in the other services.The settlers are engaged generally in the activities like agriculture, manufacturing, processing, construction, trade and commerce and fishing. The Nicobarese, on the other hand, depend on the coconut plantation and rearing of pigs for their livelihood. The other tribals are forest dwellers and food gatherers.

The population of A & N Islands comprise people from different religions, faiths and regions. The inter-caste,inter-religion and inter-region marriages are common in these islands. It is rightly said that A & N Islands, because of its special population characteristics, is a mini India.

Table 3. 8
Working and Non-Working Population of A & N Islands

Sl.No.	Heading/ population	Male No.	Male %	Female No.	Female %	Total No.	Total %
1.	Cultivation	17,411 (89.2)	21.2	2,103 (10.8)	12.7	19,514 (100)	19.7
2.	Industry	20,999 (90.4)	25.5 (9.6)	2,232 (100)	13.5	23,231	23.5
3.	Livestock	10,691	12.9	718	4.3	11,409	11.5
4.	Trade & Commerce	12,575	15.3	841	5.1	13,416	13.6
5.	Government & Other Services	20,641 (65.9)	25.1	10,690 (34.1)	64.4	31,331 (100)	31.7
	Total Workers	82,317 (83.2)	100	16,584 (16.8)	100	98.901 (100)	100
	Non Workers	72,052 (39.6)		1,09,708 (60.4)		1.81,760 (100)	
	Total	1,54,369 (55.0)		1,26.292 (45.0)		2,80,661 (100)	

Source : Compiled from the Census Reports

4

TOURISM ATTRACTIONS

A profile about A&N Islands and the population characteristics of this territory has been discussed in the previous chapters. Whether a particular place is a tourist destination or not depends on the basis of various types of attractions possessed by the place. A dissatisfied tourist is like a dangerous turndown friend who will spoil the image of the destination. Tourism attractions form the basis for the planners to plan, to make schemes for the development of tourism and so on.

The tourism attractions of A&N Islands are classified into four types, namely, natural, religious, social and cultural attractions and places of tourist interest.

1. **Natural Attractions**
   (a) Climate
   (b) Scenic Beauty
   (c) Flora and Fauna

2. **Religious Attractions**
   (a) Temples
   (b) Churches
   (c) Mosques
   (d) Gurudwaras
   (e) Others

3. **Social and Cultural Attractions**

(a) Local Lifestyle
(b) Fairs and Festivals
(c) Commercial and Industrial Units
(d) Educational Institutions
(e) Light and Sound Programme
(f) Cinema Halls

4. Places of Interest

(a) Port Blair City
Cellular Jail
Andaman Water Sports Complex
Children's Traffic Park
Gandhi Park
Marina Park
Carbyn's Cove Beach
Chatham Saw Mill
Anthropological Museum
Fisheries Museum
Mini Zoo
Cottage Industries Emporium
Samudhrika
Gymkhana Ground

(b) Wandoor Beach
(c) Viper Island
(d) Chiddiatappu
(e) Mount Harriet
(f) Cinque Island
(g) Madhuban
(h) Mahatma Gandhi National Marine Park (Jollybouy and Red Skin)
(i) Ross Island
(j) Sippighat
(k) Neil Island
(l) Havelock
(m) Long Island
(n) Rangat

(o) Barren Island
(p) Mayabunder
(q) Diglipur

NATURAL ATTRACTIONS

This is the real asset of any country/tourist destination and it requires no investment. Natural attractions are the pollution-free attractions which attract the tourists in plenty to these islands. The geology and topography of A&N Islands itself are the most beautiful attractions. The natural attractions of these islands are divided into three types as discussed below :

Climate : Climate is a factor that vitally affects tourism industry particularly in A & N Islands.. The best climate/ season to visit A & N Islands is from October to May. Approximately, these islands get rainfall for a minimum of five months and a maximum of six months. The south west monsoon commences in the beginning of May and continues till mid October. Then, from mid October, north east monsoon starts and continues till the mid December. When compared with south west monsoon, north east monsoon brings less rain. The period between January and April is full of sunlight and warmth. Foreign tourists like this climate and during this season/climate, the foreigners enjoy sunbath on the sea shore for sometime and they go for seabath. Of course, the Indian tourists also visit these islands during this climate. But the Indian tourists like the climate of cloud-less sunlight, pleasant cool weather which prevails generally during the time between October to December. During this period, the tourists need not worry about rain; weather is very pleasant, cool breeze blows and sea remains very calm. Visiting Inter Islands by boat/ ship during this season/climate is really wonderful. Tourists can witness the friendly fishes (human brained), dolphins coming in groups and their beautiful swimming, jumping and other naughty activities They accompany the boat to some distance.

Scenic Beauty : The hills, ups and downs of these Islands carry greater part of the scenic beauty. They have superlatives, peaks, swifts, living species of plants and birds and animals like crabs. The golden sandy beaches, sparkling crystal clear sea, surrounded by beautiful mangrove forests, thick rainy forests are the nature's gift to these islands. Once a tourist goes into the forest (not reserved one) he will forget himself and can enjoy the taste of peace. The coral reefs, underwater marine life, multicolour fishes, seaweed's plants and flowers make these islands as dreamland and the facility is provided by administration as a way to reach this dreamland. Tourists from different parts of the country enjoy the scenic beauty of the lush green forests.

Another attraction of the place lies with its creeks and sanctuaries. Travelling through the creeks, surrounded by the thick mangrove forests, really makes the tourists happy and cheerful. These creeks are suitably located for film shooting. The scenic view from one end to another with some Island/ Islands as background has its own beauty, which cannot be seen elsewhere in the world. As a resource, this scenic resource (natural resource) has not at all been touched for exploitation for any commercially productive purposes. This area is open to the researchers as well.

The important creeks are:

1. Wright Myo in SouthAndaman
2. Baratang in South Andaman
3. Uttara in Middle Andaman
4. Yeratta in Middle Andaman
5. Kalighat in North Andaman
6. Parangara in North Andaman

Next to the creeks, sanctuaries draw a lot of tourists. Sanctuaries are vital for preservation of its fragile eco-system. In A & N Islands there are 94 sanctuaries. Some sanctuaries are inhabited and the others uninhabited. The songs of different birds, beauty of their structure, their way of life which can be seen in these sanctuaries is all really worth watching.

In particular, tourists get excellent scenic beauty from some particular spots. Starting from the Cellular Jail, top terraces of the wing which is adjacent to the hospital offer a good scenic view. All India Radio (Protected area) is situated in Delanipur village. From the car parking place inside the AIR, the tourists can see the sea, hills, forests, trees, islands, fascinating landscape, plantation, etc. Likewise views from Mount Harriet, Carbine's Cove Tower Hill, Police Line Hill, North Bay light house, Car Nicobar, Nancowry and Chowra are really worth seeing.

Flora and Fauna : Flora and fauna of every place have a different role to play in the development of the tourism industry. Everything created by God has its own importance. From a small ant to a big elephant, a small rose plant to a big tree, chiddia to peacock and from monkey to man have their roles assigned by God. Forests of A&N Islands are unique in character and possess enormous biological diversity. Out of 15000 flowering plants in India 2200 species are found in this lush green paradise, of which 200 species (about 10%) are endemic in these islands and 1300 species are not found on the mainland. At present about 40 species are harvested for the commercial purposes. Almost all types of flowers are planted in each and every park situated in different places of A & N Islands.

As far as the fauna in these oceanic islands is concerned, about 55 species of mammals and 255 species of birds have been recorded in these islands. This is out of 350 species of mammals and 1200 species of birds found in India. Some of the endemic, endangered species of mammals include the Nicobar crabs, Andaman wild pig and a few species of rodants and bats. The avifauna is spectacular with a number of endemic endangered species such as the Andaman Teal, Narcondum Hornbill, Nicobar Megapode, Nicobar piegon, etc. There is a large influx of migrant coastal and shallow water sea birds. There are many introduced and wild mammals namely spotted deer, barking deer, goats and feral elephants, which attract the visitors.

Forests occupy about 86% (7144 sq. kms.) of the land area in A & N Island. Floristically, the forests have been classified into the following types (H G Champion and S K Seth): 1. Giant evergreen forests 2. Andaman tropical evergreen forests 3. Southern Hill top tropical evergreen forests 4. Andaman Semi-ever green forests 5. Andaman moist Deciduous forests. 6. Cane brakes 7. Bamboo brakes 8. Littoral forests 9. Tidal swamp forests.

Timber of a vast variety is available in plenty in the forests. Timber in A & N Island is divided into first class, second class and third class. Under first class, Padauk (Pteracarpus dalbergiodes), Koko (Alblzzia Lebbek), Chuglum (Terminaija bialstra and Myrstica Irya), Marble wood and satin wood are included; under second class, Pyinma Lagerstroema Flos Reginae, Bombay, Chai, Lakuch, Lalchini Pongyet, Tritmin, Mowha, Khaya, gangaw, Thingam (Hopea Odorata) are included; and under the third class, Dida Ywengyi, Toungpeingyi and Gurjan(Disterocarpus Turbinaters) are included.

RELIGIOUS ATTRACTIONS

The religious personality of A & N islands is very complex since it is a mini India. People of different religions from different states have been living in this territory besides the aborigins of this place. Hindus, Muslims, Christians, Sikhs, Buddhists, Jains, Bhahais etc., are the major religions of these islands. The people from major religions go to their respective centres daily. One more point to be mentioned here is that some people, with inborn qualities go to all the religious centres and worship all gods irrespective of their religion. Tourists of every religion go to their religious centre, temple, church, mosque, gurudwara, etc., The lists of the temples, mosques, churches etc. with their particulars are given as follows :

Table 4.1
Particulars About Hindu Temples

Sl.No.	Name of the Temple	Address
1.	Sri Laxmivinayakar	Aberdeen Bazar, Port Blair, Near TSG & AKT Bros shops.
2.	Sri Karpaga Vinayakar	Goalghar, Port Blair.
3.	Sri Vinayakar	Dairy Farm Junction, Port Blair.
4.	Sri Vetrimalai Murugan	RGT Road, Near Gandhi Park, Port Blair.
5.	Lord Shiva	South Point, Port Blair.
6.	Sri Radha Govinda	RGT Road, Near Shri Vetrimalai Murugan Temple, Port Blair.
7.	Sri Laxminarayana	Aberdeen Bazar, Port Blair.
8.	Lord Rama	Aberdeen Basti, Port Blair
9.	Lord Rama	Kumrakathi, Port Blair.
10.	Lord Iyyappan	Bhuniathapath, Port Blair.
11.	Lord Iyyappan	Sippighat, Port Blair.
12.	Lord Rama	Haddo, Port Blair.
13.	Lord Shiva	Delanipur, Port Blair.
14.	Lord Eswar & Lord Sitaram	Dairy Farm, Port Blair.
15.	Lord Hanuman	Aberdeen Bazar, Port Blair.
16.	Lord Marriamman	Austinabad, Port Blair.
17.	Lord Alaikadal Iyyanar	South Point, Port Blair.
18.	Sri Kali	Prem Nagar, Port Blair.
19.	Sri Padam Primval	Police Line, Port Blair.
20.	Sri Valmigi	Prem Nagar, Port Blair
21.	Sri Murugan	Mayabunder, North Andaman.
22.	Sri Murugan	Diglipur, North Andaman.
23.	Sri Dhandayuthapani	Garacharama, Port Blair.

Source : Personal Collections.

Table 4.2
Particulars About Mosques

Sl.No.	Name of the Mosque	Address
1.	Police Masjid	Aberdeen Bazar, Port Blair.
2.	Jama Masjid	Aberdeen Basti, Port Blair.
3.	Junglighat Masjid	Junglighat, Port Blair.
4.	Masjid	Delanipur Basti, Port Blair.
5.	Masjid	Phoniex Bay, Port Blair.

Source : Personal Collections.

Table 4.3
Particulars About Churches

Sl.No.	Name of the Church	Address
1.	Roman Catholic	Phoniex Bay, Port Blair.
2.	Ceylon Pentecot	Phoniex Bay, Port Blair.
3.	Church of North India	Phoniex Bay, Port Blair.
4.	Marthoma	Phoniex Bay, Port Blair.
5.	Indian Pentecostal	Phoniex Bay, Port Blair.
6.	Methodist	Goal Ghar, Port Blair.
7.	Yuva Shakthi	South Point/Shadipur, Port Blair.
8.	Seventh Day Adventist	Mission Dairy Farm, Port Blair.
9.	Orthodox Syrian	Phoniex Bay, Port Blair.

Table 4.4
Particulars About Other Religious Centres

Sl.No.	Name of the Centre	Address
1.	Police Gurudwaras	Aberdeen Bazar, Port Blair.
2.	Dr. Dewan Singh Gurudwara	Backside of the State Bank of India (Main Branch), Port Blair.
3.	M.E.S. Gurudwara	M.E.S. Area, Port Blair.
4.	Bahais Temple	Phoniex Bay, Port Blair.
5.	Buddhist Temple	Pongichang Area, Port Blair.

Source : Personal Collections.

SOCIAL AND CULTURAL ATTRACTIONS

Social and cultural activities, the working tangible assets, of the A&N Islands are the most important motivating and influencing factors on the tourists to visit these islands. The mixed culture and social life of the people of A&N Islands attracts the majority of the tourists who have a desire to see something new and visualise something different from their own experience. The A&N Islands is a new world, owned by India, having different patterns of life, manners, habits, social traditions, cultural traditions, hospitality, peace, festivals, etc., with attractive sites and scenes.

Local Life Style : Social and cultural development and the tourism development are interrelated. Social and cultural development attract more tourists and tourism is an important medium of social and cultural development. A&N islands is a place where people from all states of India are living. They are from different religions and they live in perfect harmony. Tourists can study the social and cultural life of this territory. The local society of these islands consists of three groups, namely, local borns, settlers and government employees, etc. Local borns are the descendants of the convicts and the freedom fighters who came in to these islands before the year 1942. Settlers are the group of people who have migrated after 1947 as a result of the partition of the country and also those who were subsequently rehabilitated by the A & N Administration. Government employees are the group of people who came here on appointment. All these groups are mixing freely with one another cutting across caste and religious boundaries. The importance of religions and regions among these three groups is slightly disappearing because marriages between people of north and south are becoming more common. For example a Hindu or Muslim from north will marry a Christian or Muslim of south and the like. All regional and religious functions are celebrated in almost all the families. On private functions like marriages, birthdays, grahapravesham and anniversaries etc., one can find all people from all religions and regions. They socialise frequently every day, or once in a week. There are many temples, churches, gurdwaras, mosques etc., for each religious group. But people visit and worship all the religious centers irrespective of whether he/she is Hindu/Muslim/ Christian, etc. Socio-cultural life of these Islands attracts many researchers to concentrate and study the areas of the peculiar life of the people of this territory.

Fairs and Festivals : Fairs and festivals are always associated with joy and happiness. Fairs and festivals are the best way of entertaining the people of all age groups since these are occasions on which they gather, assemble, exchange their views, work together, worship their god, etc. This has been an important part of the human life since olden days. Fairs and festivals have important role to play in the field of tourism. Many tourists would like to stay back for a week to enjoy the fairs and festivals. They claim that this way, they gain a lot of relief and relaxation for their own problems and obtain a lot of self satisfaction. In this tourists' paradise fairs and festivals are celebrated in almost all parts. Generally, fairs are related to government programmes as Islands on March, Trade Fairs, Navy Mela exhibition etc. As far as the festivals are concerned the A & N Administration celebrates one important festival namely Andaman Tourism Festival. The remaining festivals are celebrated by the people of the concerned religious groups. No doubt, all religions celebrate their own festivals according to their economic condition and their own style. But people from all religious groups participate without any hesitation. The most important thing is - the boys from Muslim, Christian, Sikh communities participate in all activities at the time of Hindu festivals and boys following Hindu, Christian, Sikh religions participate in all activities in Muslim festivals and the same manner in Christian festivals and so on. During such festivals Hindu orators are called and requested to talk about the Holy Kuran, Holyman Md. Nabi, Fathima, Islamism etc., and Muslim orators about Hindu almighty Gita, etc. This is really wonderful which could be seen only in A & N Islands, and a tourist can really enjoy the socio-cultural integrated festivals. Besides the religious festivals like Deepavali, Ramzan, Christmas etc., among the popular festivals, the most important festivals are linked with Hindu culture, traditions and faith.

These include :

1. Ganesh Puja
2. Panguni Uttatam
3. Mariamman Thiruvizha
4. Durga Puja
5. Kali Puja
6. Saraswati Puja

7. Ram Navami
8. Gokula Astami
9. Gurunanak Jayanti
10. Nag Panchami
11. Holi
12. Diwali
13. Pongal
14. Christmas
15. Ramzan
16. Shivarathri
17. Vasanth Panchami
18. Ramleela.

Ganesh Puja : Ganesh Puja is celebrated on "Chathurthi Thithi" every year. People from the south call this puja "Vinayaka Chathurthi". The image of Lord Ganesh is made out of black clay with a lot of glittering decoration. People buy the Ganesh image in a size according to their economic conditions. The Ganesh temples at Aberdeen Bazar, Goal Ghar etc., are beautifully decorated and special pujas or 'Arti' are performed by the priests, Iyers or pujaris in honour of Lord Ganesh. Of all the Ganesh temples, Sri Lakshmi Vinayagar temple at Aberdeen Bazar and Karpaga Vinyagar at Goalghar are the chief attractions on the occasion. Generally, the puja is celebrated for three days. The temples are full of devotees (Bhakth). During puja, people offer "Kozhukattai' and "Sundal" to the deity "Vinyagar", and after the puja these kozhukattai and sundals are distributed among the gatherings. Some organisations and offices or groups of people also perform common puja. A big image of Lord Ganesh is made. An important place in the village or the organization is decorated with pandals and puja and 'Arti' are performed. The third day the image is taken round in the village and city in procession with dance and songs and is immersed into the sea. All the three days the temples are full of devotees. The people from other religions also visit the temple with their family members.

Panguni Utthiram : This is the biggest and the most important festival in these islands. This festival is celebrated to honour the Lord Sri Vetrimalai Murugan (Lord Karthik), a son of Siva and Parvathi. Sri Vetrimalai (victory hill) Murugan Temple is the oldest temple in these islands. Now a new Kalyana Mandapam (two floors) has been constructed and renovation work of the main temple has also been completed. The important feature of this temple is that the people of all regions and religions of our country and foreign tourists visit this temple. The strong belief of the people is that their requests are fulfilled and graced by the Lord Murugan. During the festival, the temple is decorated with a lot of colour lights etc. This Uttiram festival is celebrated every year during the Tamil month of panguni, in full moon day covering the "Uttira Natachitram", for a period of ten days. During the festival, every day of the period of celebration, 'Anna Dhanam' is given.

About 10000 to 15000 people come to the temple to the get Anna Dhanam (i.e they eat full meal). On the last day of the celebration called "Thee Mithi" people and devotees whose requests are granted by the powerful Sri Vetrimalai Murugan wear "Sedal Ornaments" on their body, face, tongue etc., with "Kavadies". Among the kavadies, "Arugandam Kavadies" and "Parakkam Kavadies" are really very difficult to carry. People from other islands come to Port Blair to participate this celebration. People on the roads to see them. All religious people offer lime and orange juice, salted sweet water, butter milk, and water to all the devotees, visitors, tourists etc., as a partial fulfilment of their promises. The sedal and kavady bearers walk on fire (Thee Mithi) and reach the "Moolasthanam". One cannot stand near the fire even at a distance of six metres. Devotees walk on the fire which means everybody should accept the supreme power of the Lord Sri Vetrimalai Murugan.

Sri Marriamman Thiruvizha Festival : This is the second biggest festival of the Hindus celebrated in honour of Goddess Arulmigu Sri Marriamman. This temple is situated in Austinabad village, at a distance of six kms from Port Blair

Bus Terminus on Chiddiyatappu route. The belief of all the people from all religions is that Goddess Mariamma has been guarding these islands. There is an incident, narrated by the devotees as it is a real one. When the Dhannikari Dam was constructed, the contractor could not complete it successfully due to frequent cracks and scratches, etc. Then he prayed to Goddess Marriamman by wearing sedal ornaments and he saw her in his dream and she encouraged him to continue his efforts. The following week he could successfully complete the whole dam. After the completion of the dam, the contractor constructed the present temple (RCC building) and deposited some amount of money in the temple's name for the everyday puja, celebrations and maintenance. Now all visit this temple and worship the Goddess Mariamman irrespective of their religions. The tourists, including foreigners, do not leave these islands without worshipping these two temples. The festival is celebrated every year during the month of February. For Goddess Marriaman also, the devotees perform puja and Arti in the same manner to God Sri Vetrimalai Murugan. Theemithi, Arugandam kavadi, Parakkum kavadi, Pal kavadi Paneer kavadi, Ilaneer kavadi are the special attractions for the people, devotees and tourists.

Sashti Festival : This is celebrated in honour of Sri Vetrimalai Murugan immediately after the Deepavali for a period of six days since God Murugan has six faces popularly known as "Arumugam" i.e, each day is meant for one face. During these days, Laxcharchanas and special pujas/artis are performed in the temple. Devotees purchase Laxarchana tickets costing Rs. 101/-. Tourists visit these islands during this festival period, purchase tickets, participate in puja and take the prasad to their native village/country as a divine symbol of Sri Vetriamalai Murgan.

Durga Puja : This is also an important festival of Hindus celebrated with great enthusiasm. Though the Hindus from all regions participate, the Hindus from Calcutta (West Bengal) take the full responsibility of its celebration in these islands. This puja is celebrated by all the Hindus in the name of Navarathri puja for nine days. Every year Durga puja is celebrated in these islands during September-October. Bengali associations in each village and some organisations make the image of goddess Durga in highly decorative manner out of clay along with the images of other gods namely, Sri Ganesh, Sri Karthik (Sri Murugan) etc., and they perform puja with the help of pandits. On Vijayadhasami i.e on the tenth day, the images are taken out in procession to various places near Haddo jetty, Aberdeen jetty for immersion in the sea. A large crowd assembles near the Goalghar, Junglighat Junction, Dairyfarm, Schoolline Junction, Dilanipur, Haddo etc., to witness the procession for immersion.

Ram Navmi : It is celebrated in honour of the birthday of Lord Rama by performing special puja and arti only in Ram temples located in Aberdeen Basthi, Kumrakheti, Haddo and Dairy Farm. Temples are decorated with colourful lights and musical instruments are played. Songs on Lord Rama and Sita are also sung.

Gokulaashtami : It is celebrated in the name of the birthday of Lord Krishna who is regarded as the eighth incarnation of Lord Vishnu. This festival is celebrated in August-September. In Radha Krishna, Radha Govindha temples on RGT Road, Sri Krishna Temple in Dairy Farm, Radhakrishna Temple in Junglighat, this festival is celebrated with great enthusiasm. Temples are fully illuminated with lights and coloured lamps. Group bhajans/group songs on Krishna, continuous puja performance with loud clappings and sayings like "Krishna Ki Jay" and other performances continue till midnight when Sri Krishna took birth. After the birth puja, prasadhams made out of sweet sooji, sweet boonthi, cut bananas, and sugarcane etc. are distributed. All temples are crowded with devotees and other people.

Sri Guru Nanak Jayanthi : This is celebrated by the Punjabis.

It commemorates the birthday of Sri Guru Nanak. This festival is celebrated on 25th November of every year, with great enthusiasm. Police Gurudwara in Aberdeen Bazar, Dr. Diwan Singh Gurudwara behind the State Bank of India, Main Branch, Gurudwara in MES area are illuminated with beautiful colour lamps. Songs, prayers, readings, bhajans etc., are the special features on the occasion. They organise a simple but excellent procession with the songs and bhajans with the call of "Guru Nanakji ki jay".

Saraswathi Puja : Saraswathi puja is another festival celebrated by people, educational institutions and other organizations put up and is associated with the worship of Maa Saraswathi, the goddess of education and *vidhai* (vidhya) knowledge. Big pandals are put up at the important places in the city. The image of goddess Sri Saraswathi with *vina* sitting on white colour lotus kept in the pandal. Continuous puja, *arti* are performed throughout the day. Next day, the image of goddess is taken in procession, accompanied with dances and songs to the Haddo jetty, Aberdeen jetty or Chatham jetty for the immersion.

Sri Kali Puja : This festival is associated with the worship of Maa Kali as the destroyer of the evils. This festival is celebrated in the months of October-November every year. The Bengalis take keen interest and celebrate it enthusiastically. The image of Maa Kali showing her angry action of killing a Rakchashan is installed at different places. Kali temple at Prem Nagar is decorated with coloured lamps. Prescribed pujas and artis are performed. Hindus, particularly Bengalis, visit this temple and other places where the images of the goddess are installed and worshipped. Next day, the image is taken in procession with songs and dances to Haddo Jetty, Aberdeen Jetty and Junglighat Jetty for the immersion. A large crowd assembles to witness the procession at Goal Ghar, opposite State Library, Junglighat Junction, Dairfarm Junction, Aberdeen Bazar, Dilanipur, Haddo, etc.

Sri Shiva Rathri : This is another important festival celebrated in this island. This is celebrated for one day during the month of February-March in honour of the auspicious day of the Lord Shiva's marriage with the goddess Parvathi. The temples of Lord Shiva in South Point, Delanipur, Phar Goan, Garacharma perform special pujas and artis with the usual decorations. In Sri Vetrimalai Murugan Temple the Shiva Lingam is specially adorned with colourful flowers. In all the Shiva temples, the bhajans, kirthanas, songs, speeches, talks, dramas, video films on Shivaparvathi continue throughout the night. After early morning puja, *prasatham* is distributed among the devotees.

Holi : This is celebrated as a festival of colours during the months of February-March. In this territory, the Holi is celebrated by the people of all age groups irrespective of the religions and regions. In each and every village, a 'holika' made out of coconut leaves, and other firewood is burnt during the midnight Then, from the early morning itself, the sprinkling of colour (powder and water) from men to men, women and among children starts. This activity goes upto 1.00 pm. After that the people go to Carbynscove beach for bathing. After taking bath, the people come out of their houses, wearing new clothes, go and meet their friends, embrace each other, take sweets and blessings from elders etc. Some people go to temples and the other youngsters usually go to watch cinema.

Prakash Yathra : This is celebrated just a day before Christmas by going in a procession. The Christians participate in the celebration. Both males and females participate and each of them carries a lighted candle saying some hymns from Bible. The procession is held in a calm and peaceful manner.

Other Festivals : Among other Hindu, festivals like Nag Panchami Pongal, Deepavali, Ram Leela, Vasantha Panchami etc., celebrated in these islands Deepavali, the festival of lights is most important. Every house, irrespective of religions and regions. celebrate Deepavali by wearing new clothes, preparing and distributing by firing crackers etc. On Deepavali day, people take oil bath and wear new, colourful clothes. During evening hours, the houses are decorated with lighted candles or series of lights. Next to Deepavali, Maha Karthiakai, the festival in honour of god Sri Murugan, the god of knowledge and courage, is of importance. On this festival also the houses are decorated with lighted candles. The elders undertake fasting, younger ones enjoy the crackers during the evening hours, Sri Vetrimalai Murugan temple is illuminated with lights which should not be missed by the tourists. Apart from the festivals of the Hindus, Christians and Sikhs, there are also some festivals which are celebrated among other communities living in these islands. These include Jains who celebrate the birthday of Lord Parasanth and Mahaveer. Buddhists celebrate Buddha Jayanthi, Muslims celebrate Muharram, Ramzan Bakrid, etc.

Commerce and Industry : Commercial and industrial development of A & N islands plays an important role in the growth of tourism industry. Though the commercial and industrial units are scattered over the inhabited islands, majority of the units are located in the Port Blair city. The Port Blair city is famous for its handicrafts like shell-made items.

The prospects for setting up of such units in these islands are encouraging. The present important trade centres are Aberdeen Bazar, Diglipur, Junglighat, Middle Point, Bambooflat, Ferrargunj, Rangat, Mayabunder, Campbell Bay.

Educational Institutions : In this territory, there are only two colleges—Jawaharlal Nehru Government College in Port Blair and Mahatma Gandhi Government College in Mayabunder. These colleges offer arts, science and commerce courses at degree and post graduate levels. Government B.Ed College is in Port Blair.

The literacy rate of A&N islands is - male 78.99%, female 65.46% and overall 73.02% as per the 1991 census whereas the same in Port Blair city is 86.59%, 75.08% and 81.69% respectively. There are about 340 educational institutions in A&N islands including about 70 institutions in Nicobar islands.

Light and Sound Programme : There is light and sound programme run at Cellular Jail, a national memorial. The programme, in Hindi and English, is shown during evening hours everyday.

Cinema Halls : In A & N Islands except Port Blair, the islands do not have commercial cinema halls. In Port Blair there are six cinema halls located at different places at a distance of l-4 kms. from the Bus Teminus. Most of the halls hold only two shows every day and three on Saturdays and Sundays and there are four to five shows festivals as well. All the halls screen the Tamil, Hindi and Telugu films. Sometimes, some cinema halls also show Malayalam, Bengali and English films.

PLACES OF INTEREST

Port Blair City : This is the only city in the A & N Islands. Port Blair is the nerve centre of the econony of the Islands. Port Blair is located in the south-east portion of South Andaman division. The city derives its name from Archibald Blair, a brilliant surveyor who was commissioned by the British Government in the 18th century for a penal settlement. It is the capital of A & N Islands. Port Blair is an important harbour in the islands, handling most of their cargo & passenger traffic.The city has airport which receives passengers by Boeing 737 of Indian Airlines. Now the flight is operated by Alliance Ltd, a subsidiary company of Indian Airlines. The total geographical area of the town is 7.9 sq.kms. It has 57 revenue villages with a population of 74,955 as per 1991 census. About 26.7% of total population of A & N Islands is living in this city. The occupational aspect of the city is divided into five categories namely government employees, school and college teachers, owners of small scale industrial units, trades, skilled workers and labourers etc. Taxis, government transport buses are the only modes of travel. The Port Blair city has a number of tourist attractions and places of historic interest and significance; its scenic beauty attracts a large number of tourists both from mainland and abroad. The important places and places of tourist interest in Port Blair city are described as below :

Cellular Jail : The Cellular Jail is a national memorial. It is located in Port Blair two kms. from Bus Terminus. This is known as Bastile of India and relic of bygone years where India's freedom fighters were incarcerated. Every molecule of the wall and floor has a harrowing tale to tell. The construction of the Cellular Jail had been started in 1896 and was completed in 1906. The Jail acquired the name 'Cellular' because it is entirely made up of individual cells for the solitary confinement of the prisoners. Originally, the Cellular Jail was a seven wing, puce coloured building with a Central Tower acting as its fulcrum and a massive structure comprising honeycomb like corridors. Each wing is three storyed with many cells. All the seven wings vary in length but the width and the height were symmetrical and were 28ft and 40ft respectively. The size of each cell is 13 x 7 ft without any dormitory. The storeys and cells tell the tales of the sufferings, sacrifices and indomitable courage of freedom fighters who were transported to the penal settlement are for reference. Due to an earthquake, four wings were damaged, and at present only three out of seven prongs are intact. The damaged portions have been left for the construction of a hospital. Hence the G.B.Pant hospital is functioning there.

The patriots, who raised voice against the British, were sent to this jail where many perished. Freedom fighters like Veer Savarkar, Baba Prithvi Singh Azad, Bhai Parmanand, Ullash Kar Datta, T. Sachidanada Sivam, and host of others faced inhuman torture at the hands of David Barrie and other jailors.

The Cellular Jail has now been declared a National Monument. The saga of this heroic struggle is now brought alive in a moving sound and light show. There the department of tourism runs shows based on the history of this island and jail as if it is told by the oldest "peepal tree", still living inside the jail. Timings to the Cellular Jail during all days is between 9 am to 5 pm with a lunch break between 12 noon to 1 pm.

Andaman Water Sports Complex (AWSC) : AWSC is situated in Aberdeen Jetty, just one km from Port Blair Bus Terminus. Walking around the AWSC gives a pleasant feeling, pleasant breeze, a wonderful sight of glittering waves to a tourist. This is a unique sports complex in India and of its own kind. The safe water sports facilities include Rowing Boats, Paddle Boats, Kayaks, Aquacycle, Aqua-glide, Bumper Boats, the Gemini Boats, Para Sailing, Sail Boats, Wind-Surfacing, Speed Boats, Glass bottom boats etc. The complex has a saline water swimming pool, Food-Plaza, change room, toilet and Children Traffic Park. The Complex is open all days. Timings for the Safe Water Sports is 8 am to 8 pm. and for Adventure Water Sports 8 am to 5 pm.

Children's Traffic Park : The newly built Children Traffic Park is very beautiful looking. All the traffic rules are depicted on the wall in bold pictures. The pillars with different traffic lights in small sizes, speed breakers, small mile stones, cemented roads etc. have been constructed. At present the children practise bicycle, tri-cycle, baby motor riding etc., inside the park. All vehicles are available for hire. The tourism department is managing this park. They charge Re.1 per head as entry fee and Rs.2 per vehicle as hire charge for the duration of an hour. This park is set up with a view to educate young children the traffic rules.

Gandhi Park : This is another beautiful park in Port Blair city near Sri. Vetrimalai Murugan Temple. This park has been set up on the bank of Thilthaman Water Tank. Gandhi Park is just 1 km from Port Blair Bus Terminus.The park has all the facilities including children's park, amusement park, entertainment park, deer park, water sports, nature walk, lake garden and a marvellous restaurant. Gandhi Park has been constructed by keeping Japanese Temple in the centre. Tourists enjoy the colourful lamps during evening hours.This park is full of tourists during evening hours particularly on sundays. The Thilthaman Tank was once the only source of drinking water to the Port Blair city. The park is open all days.

Marina Park : This is a colourful park of national importance. Netaji Subhash Chandra Bose's statue is erected inside this park. Colourful flowers, beautiful looking garden, a small children park, a semi-canteen, illuminative lightings etc., are the special features of this park. This park is situated within 1 km from Port Blair Bus Terminus. The park is full of visitors during evening hours every day. Tourists can go around at any time during the day. Recently a new restaurant has been attached with this park for tourists. Since this park is connected with the Children's Traffic Park and Aberdeen Water Sports Complex, this park is seen as a red stone in a ring.

Carbyn's Cove Beach : This beach is within 7 kms from Port Blair Bus Terminus towards south-east direction. Carbyn's Cove Beach is one of the most beautiful picturesque sea beaches of A & N Islands. This beach is named after Reverent. H.Corbyn, the chaplain of the settlement. Just in front of the beach, a hotel named as Peerless Resort (previously named as Andaman Beach Resort) provides quality food, water sports facilities including diving. One more restaurant namely ' the wave' provides open air bar facility. The Carbyn's Cove Beach provides a beautiful scenic view, marvellous sun-rise and moon-rise. Tourists can enjoy fully the natural beauty of the A & N Islands. This beach is fully decorated with the sodium vapour lamps. This is a sandy beach and an ideal place for swimming. The foreign tourists enjoy their sunbath, moonbath, and starbath when there is no moon. This is an excellent beach for picnicking. The Carbyn's Cove Beach can rightly be called as 'Kovalam' of A & N Islands. The coconut nursery in Carbyn's Cove is worth seeing. The Agriculture Department has opened a sales counter for tender coconut at a very low rate at the beach. Every year on Chaitra Pournamy (Buddha Poornima) night, the beach is full of tourists.

Chatham Saw Mill : The Chatham Saw Mill is one of the largest saw mills in Asia. This is situated in Chatham Island about 4 kms from Port Blair Bus Terminus. It is a separate island connected with Port Blair by road. This mill has two big cranes called EOT cranes which are used for both stacking and feeding. The wood workshop of this mill is worth seeing. This saw mill functions as a store-house of timber like Padauk, Gürjan, Marble Satine wood etc. Here the tourists can see some of the world's best species of timber and transformed into various sizes use for by railways, ship-building and other manufacturing industries. The Chatham Island has the second largest wharf of these islands and Island-Mainland plying ships are berthed here. The tourists can go around the mill at any time on all working days.

Anthropological Museum : This museum is situated within 1.25kms. from Port Blair bus terminus on Haddo via Phoenix Bay route. This museum displays the tools, instruments, models and habitats of the tribals named Great Andamanese, Jarawas, Sentinalese, Onges, Nicobaries and Shompens. The arts and handicrafts of these tribals are very attractive and induce the tourists to think seriously about the art and culture of the tribals. This display provides rare opportunity to the Indian as well as foreign tourists to compare today's space age with the stone-age. Such arts are providing some basic ideas to our present day artisans to produce various handicrafts. This museum is open to tourists all days.

Fisheries Museum : This is situated, surrounded by Marina Park, Andaman Water Sports Complex, and Children Traffic Park, within 1.5kms from Port Blair bus terminus. It exhibits species of marine life peculiar to the islands, Indo-Pacific and Bay of Bengal. Over 350 species of marine life are very carefully preserved in this museum. It gives an intellectual insight to the both domestic and foreign tourists about the nature and character of marine life and wealth in these islands. At present it is called Marine museum. Tourists are allowed to visit the museum during the working hours on all working days.

Mini Zoo : There is no big zoo in these islands except the Mini Zoo which is situated about 2.5 kms. from Port Blair bus terminus on Chatham route. The tourists are specially fascinated by the birds of the world's rarest species that are found here. Some of them are:-

Nicobar Pigeon
-Emerald Dove
Megapode
Black Myana
Imperial Pigeon
Parakeet
Andaman Cuckoo
Nicobar Cuckoo
Teal, etc.

The salt water crocodile rearing farm is a special attraction to the tourists. Timings to visit the Mini Zoo are from 7 am to 12 noon and from 13 pm to 17 pm on all working days.

Cottage Industries Emporium : This emporium in Middle Point at a distance of about 2 kms from Port Blair bus terminus, is run by the A & N Administration through the Directorate of Industries. They function as a show room and marketing shop. All local handicrafts — woodmade, shellmade, canemade — are sold in the emporium. The prices are comparatively low. This emporium is always crowded with visitors, tourists and buyers etc. The local artisans keep their special products in the show room for sale. Foreign tourists are fond of shell items, wooden dancing dolls, and wooden walking sticks. Pen stands, night lamps, necklace, table weight, shell calendar are specially liked by the domestic tourists. Timing to visit the Cottage Industries is from 9 am to 7 pm on all working days.

Samudrika : This is a Naval Marine Musuem. It is maintained by the naval authority and situated 2 kms from Port Blair bus terminus on Haddo via Delanipur route, just opposite to Andaman Teal House. The tourists can witness here a wide variety of shells and marine life in A & N Islands. A good collection of literature is displayed on special wall boards (write ups) and models are the special features of this Samudrika. A good collection of shells, corals, fishes, snakes, anemon fishes, bones of dangerous fishes, drawings of different marine lives are displayed in the museum. The main purpose of the Samudrika museum is to create awareness among the people on various aspects of oceanic environment. Samudrika is open to tourists on all days during working hours except on sundays and public holidays.

Gymkhana Ground : This is a famous ground in A & N Islands, situated just opposite to Marina park. This is within 1 km from Port Blair bus terminus on Shadipur via J.N.R.M. route. This ground has the facilities of night hours play in Netaji Stadium where all the functions, parades, festivals, competitions, annual days, sports days of colleges and schools are celebrated. The initial part of the ground consists of a swimming pool of an international standard and it has been constructed recently. The central part of the ground has the Netaji Stadium and Sports Authority of India's offices etc. The last part of the ground has a newly constructed velodrome. Some foreign tourists also use the velodrome. The whole Gymkhana ground and the Marina Park are surrounded by a small railway route. The tourists can go around by the mini train, the capacity of which is about 40 passengers.

Wandoor Beach: The Wandoor beach is situated within 30 kms from Port Blair town on the west coast of South Andaman. This is a beautiful sand beach attracting domestic tourists as well as foreign tourists. Wandoor is famous for holiday picnic. Next to Carbyn's Cove, this is a suitable place for swimming and snorkling. Transparent crystal clear water with coral reef offers an exotic opportunity to observe interesting underwater life. This is an ideal place for fishing also. It offers a pictureseque landscape and an ideal place for diving. Wandoor beach is the entrance to the famous marine park named as Mahatma Gandhi Marine National Park consisting of 15 islands of which the main islands, are Jolly Bouy and Redskin, the only islands open for tourists in the National Park.

There is no ticket to go around the Wandoor beach. Wandoor has a beautiful guest house with a marvellous scenic beauty from all directions. Tourists and visitors can stay there after obtaining the permission from the forest department i.e Chief Wild Life Warden, Port Blair. For food facilities, there are small hotels situated near the bus stop. Among them, a hotel run by the Mahila Mandal of Wandoor, is worth mentioning. They offer all types of food hygienically prepared. The prices are comparitively low. This beach can be developed further.

Viper Island : Viper Island is situated at a sea distance of 2 kms each from Haddo Jetty and Junglighat Jetty. It is a separate Island. There is no road transport to the island and inside the island. Beautiful coconut plantations in the island attract tourists. Viper Island has a marvellous scenic beauty. Some say that this island is named after a snake called viper, with two heads, found in plenty in this Island. Others hold that it is the name of a particular language. But, actually, the island is named as Viper Island in memory of the vessel called T S S Viper in which Lt. Archibald Blair came to these Islands in 1876 for the establishment of a penal settlement. The vessel Viper met with an accident and was wrecked near this islands. That's why the Island is called Viper Island. As a result of the accident, the British people had chosen this island to keep all the prisoners under penal settlement before the construction of Cellular Jail. After the construction of the Cellular Jail, the women prisoners were kept in the Viper Island. The Viper Island Jail had gallows on the top of a hillock. Here in this jail, the condemned women prisoners were hanged. Though the signs of penal settlement are completely obliterated, the Jail and its gallows are retained as a tourist spot.

Chidiyatappu : The Chidlatappu is the southern most tip of the South Andaman and is situated at a distance of 28 kms from Port Blair Bus Terminus. It takes one hour to reach here from the bus terminus by bus and 30 minutes by private transport. This place is generally known as 'Bird Island'. In Hindi language 'Chidia' means 'small bird' and 'tappu' means Island. All birds migrate to this resort. Most of the species of birds found in A & N Island are found here. Chidiatappu provides a panaromic view, scenic beauty, lush green view and lovable blue oceanic view. This is the most picturesque beach for picnics and fishing. The surrounding lush green mangroves, the abundance of birds add natural touch to the whole area which attracts tourists . There is a beautiful guest house, maintained by tne Forest Department. Visitors can stay in the guest house with the prior permission of the Forest Department, Haddo, or the Chief Wild Life Warden, Port Blair. Near the guest house there are small hotels which provide good Indian food at reasonable prices. Visitors are advised to inform them in advance. They serve hot fried fish, prawn, chicken and fresh curd. Besides the hotels, a cook is also attached with the guest house.

A beautiful sand beach is within 2.75 kms. from Chidiatappu bus stop. This is situated in a place called "Munda Pahar". To reach the beach, the tourists have to trek. A road to this sand beach is being laid. At present a large number of tourists and local visitors walk through the jungle to enjoy the natural beauty. This sand beach, like Carbyn's Cove beach, has transparent, clear water of the same level upto 1/2 kms from the shore. Sitting under the shadow of the trees very near the beach and hearing the sweet songs of the 'singing chidias', twiters of swallows, screams of squirrels, coos of pigeons and cuckoos, talks and speeches of parrots and singing larks, one tends to forget himself/herself on the Chidiatappu sand beach.

Mount Harriet : It is situated within 55 kms. by road and 15 kms by sea from the Port Blair. Tourists can reach Mount Harriet in 2 hrs. by road and in about 40 min. by ferry. The sea route is from the Marine Jetty to Hope Town and from there to Mount Harriet by road. This is situated opposite Port Blair This is the second highest peak of these islands (the first one is Saddle peak). The height of the Mount Harriet is about 1200 ft. After reaching Hope Town by bus or by ferry, it will take another 80 minutes to reach the peak of the Mount Harriet. All tourists go upto the peak and enjoy the natural scenic beauty. They can see from the peak, the large part of South Andaman and other small islands like Havelock, Ross and Neil and can enjoy rare flora and fauna, endemic birds, animals, butterflies etc. As per the records, the Mount Harriet was frequantly used as summer resort by the British Chief Commissioners. The Forest Department has constructed a rest house for its own use. However, the tourists are also allowed to stay (Indian tourists can stay during night) with the permission of the Chief Wild Life Warden, Port Blair/the Forest department, Haddo. Tourists are advised to take eatables, snacks, food and water with them.

Cinque Island : This island is an uninhabited one. This is situated 35 kms. from Port Blair and has been declared a sanctuary. From Wandoor it takes 2 hrs. and from Port Blair 3 hrs. and from Chiddiatoppu 1½ hrs. to reach this island by ferry or boat. Cinque island is an enchanting one with rare corals and underwater marine life, a fine sandy beach and tropical rain forest. This beach is an excellent one for diving, snorkeling, sunbath, sand bath, etc. This island offers the lure of underwater corals ground and beautiful beach. Dolphin fishes greet the eyes. At present, no scheduled boat or ferry goes to this island but the tour conducted by the tour operator like Sagar Travels, Shompen Hotels etc., on a contract basis. The tourists can enjoy the beauty of spotted deers found in plenty in these islands. Tourists can go to the island but are not allowed to stay overnight. Tourism department offers tented accommodation facility to the tourists at a reasonable rate. Tourists are advised to carry eatables, drinking water etc., with them as nothing is available in this island to eat and drink.

Madhuban : It is a beautiful place and trekking area situated in the north east of South Andaman at a distance of 80 kms. by road from Port Blair bus terminus and 25 kms by sea from Mount Harriet. This place has a very interesting colourful view. It is a real, enchanting and enthralling sight to see the elephants which are trained to carryout different operations of log extraction in the tropical jungles of these islands. Madhuban is a very famous place for taking seabath. This area also abounds sunny and golden beaches where one can bask in the sun. Tourists can enjoy the beauty of exotic flora and fauna, endemic birds, animals, butterflies and trained elephants lumbering on, which are the most interesting part of the trek.

Mahatma Gandhi Marine National Park : This national park is situated 30 kms. from Port Blair, on south west coast of the main South Andaman Island. This park covers an area of 281.5 sq. kms. and is made up of open sea, creeks and fifteen islands. Among them, the most important islands are Jolly Bouy and Red Skin which have been opened for tourists. Tourists can go upto Wandoor by bus from Port Blair bus terminus. From Wandoor Jetty, they can avail of the water transport facilities, provided by the tourism department, Andaman & Nicobar Administration and some private tour operators to reach these islands. While going to these islands, tourists can enjoy the natural beauty of mangrove forests along with creeks and magnificent tropical forest. Jolly Bouy and Redskin islands have fascinating coral reefs and rare underwater marine life like exotic varieties of beautifully coloured coral fishes. Tourists are attracted by the fringing type of coral reefs growing around these islands. More than 50 types of corals are found in Jolly Bouy and Red Skin islands. These two islands have beautiful and excellent sandy beach with crystal clear water, colourful fishes, variety of coral reef, like clown, butterfly, surgeon, angel, parrot, bat, sea anemon, tiger, sea cucumber, special big prawn fish, etc., and overwhelm the tourists. The researchers and scientists are attracted by this natural heaven for the academic purposes as well. Besides fishes, other marine life found comprises star fishes, sea lilly, feather star, gian clam shell, troches sea cucumber, sponges and sea anemons etc. The sea transport operators offer beautiful glass bottom boats by which tourists can enjoy the beauty of underwater marine life. Andaman and Nicobar Administration charge a nominal entry fee of Re. 1.00 from Indian tourists and Rs. 2.00 from foreign tourists with a 50% concession to the children. Boat fares (subject to change) including facilities of Glass Bottom Boat from Wandoor Jetty to these Islands are as follows:-

Foreign Tourists	Indian Tourists	
Adult (per head)	Rs. 35.00	Rs.100.00
Child (per head)	Rs. 15.00	Rs. 50.00

Ross Island : This is a separate island situated in the north of Port Blair harbour and is about 200 acres in area. At present this island is under the Indian Navy. During the British period, the Ross Island was the administrative headquarter of the Andaman Nicobar Islands. It was developed into self equipped township with all facilities, required for a civilised colony. Tourists can reach this island within 20 minutes from Phoniex Jetty. The marine department operates a regular ferry service to this island daily except Wednesday. Initially, the freedom fighters of the first world war of Independence of 1857 brought to Andamans were lodged on Ross Island. Dr. James Patterson Walker, the chairman of Andaman committees, arrived in Port Blair on 10th March, 1858, and established the infamous and the dreaded penal settlement with 200 convicts. British officers lived happily with all facilities like church, bakery, hospital, bath rooms, swimming pool, tennis ground etc. But now the magnificent structure of art and architecture is in ruins. The ruins on Ross Island remind us of the pomp and glory of the bygone years. As far as the attractions are concerned small musuem named as 'smritika' has been organised and maintained by the Indian Navy. This musuem depicts the history of the

Island. Some spotted deers and peacocks are found on this island. All tourists are permitted to visit this precious Island but no one is allowed to stay overnight. No canteen or shop serving eatables, is available on Ross Island and hence the visitors are advised to take with them all the essential items like food, bread, water, tea, coffee, etc.

Sippighat : This place is situated 14 kms. from Port Blair bus terminus on the way to Wandoor. Just on the top of the Sippighat bus stand is located Sri Ayyappa Temple. Local people tourists visit this temple for prayers. The Andaman & Nicobar Administration has established an agricultural farm. The total area of this farm is 80 acres. Scientists contribute their full efforts in experimenting many new varieties of plants and species which have high potential growth in these islands. As a result of these experiments the excellent growth of clove, pepper, nutmeg, cinnamon, pinapples, papaya, oranges and bananans etc., has been achieved and it has been proved that these can be produced on a large scale in these Islands. Just nearby this farm, the Central Agricultural Research Insititute has established another experimental farm for growing coconut plants in saline water. Maximium visitors go around this farm, at present, only for the academic purpose. Tourists are allowed to go and visit this farm. Timings are from 6 am to 11.15 am and from 12 noon to 13.00 am and it is closed on Sundays and other public holidays.

Neil Island: This is a separate and beautiful island with lush green forest and sandy beaches. This is an inhabited island covering a total area of 7.3 sq. miles. Comparatively, more Bengalis inhabit here and the total population of this island is 2463 including 4 tribals as per the 1991 census. This island is situated at a distance of 45 kms. from Port Blair Phoniex Bay Jetty. The main work of the people of this island is vegetable cultivation. Maximum vegetables are sent to different islands only from Neil Island. The wholesale vegetable merchants purchase the vegetables at cheap rates and sell them Port Blair, Rangat, Mayabunder, etc., at high prices. The Neil Island can be called the "Kitchen Garden of the A & N Islands". The Island has beautiful sand beaches surrounded by the forests which attract the tourists. Among the beaches, Sitapur Beach is the most important one. This beach is surrounded by beautiful tropical rain forests. Tourists have recently started visiting this beach. The A & N Administration operates ferry service to Neil Island. Normally it takes 4-5 hrs. to reach Neil Island by boat depending upon the weather conditions. The tour operators offer chartered boats but it turns out to be expensive. The Neil Island has one accommodation, run by the tourism department, where the tourists can stay.

Havelock : This is also a separate, charming island with lush green forest and sandy beaches. This island is named after the famous Gen. Havelock. The island is partly hilly and partly plain. This is an inhabited island. The population of this island is 3681 as per 1991 census. Major part of the population is Bengalis. This island is at a distance of 57 kms. from Port Blair Phoniex, Jetty connected by ferry service. It takes five hours to reach this island from Port Blair depending upon weather conditions. The main features of this island are that the land is fertile, the beaches are natural, serene and unpolluted. The main occupation of the people of this island is cultivation of vegetables and fruits. Near the jetty, the tourist department has constructed a beautiful accommodation called Yatri Niwas. Among the beaches, the most important one is Radha Nagar beach, which attracts the tourists and is situated at a distance of about 10 kms. from Yatri Niwas. The tourist department has developed this beach with care. Tourists can enjoy the play of Dolphins, the marine life and other flying fishes etc., when they travel by ferry to this island. They can have camping facility near the Radha Nagar beach. One can also reach the beach directly from the Neil Island Jetty which is just opposite to Radha Nagar.

Long Island : This is a small inhabited island situated at a distance of 85 kms. from Port Blair, Phoniex Bay Jetty. The population of this island is 1917, mainly rural as per 1991 census. This island is connected with other places by ferry service. There is a small scale industrial unit producing plywood named Jayashree Timber products. The long island has an important beautiful unpolluted natural sandy beach called Lalaji beach surrounded by thick rain forest and coconut plantation, located at a distance of about 11 kms. by jungle trek and six kms. by sea. This beach is suitable for snorkling, diving and swimming. There are beautiful corals on this beach. Those who wish to spend days without being disturbed can go to this island and stay there. The Long Island has two guest houses one is owned by Forest department and the other by small scale unit. Tourists can stay in the Forest guest house with the prior permision from the Forest Department, Haddo. Tourists are advised to carry all eatables, essential items from the Long Island shops as nothing is available at the beach. To reach the beach, the tourist can bargain with the local fishermen for the small fishing boats, the journey by which is very interesting.

Rangat : Rangat is situated in Middle Andaman at a distance of 170 kms. by road and 93 km. by sea from Port Blair. It is the tehsil headquarter and a developing town. It takes five hours to reach Rangat from Port Blair by bus and around eight hours by boat. Rangat is very near Jarawas reserved areas. It is understood that the villages very near to reserved area are visited by the Jarawas during the night. They steal coconuts, clothes, particularly red coloured clothes, iron items, utensils, bananas etc. The population of Rangat is 33,368, mainly rural as per 1991 census. Rangat has all infrastructural facilities. The settlers are mainly Tamilians, Malayalis Bengalis, etc.

Vehicle ferrys help the transport to cross the two current water creeks namely Middle Strait Jetty and Uttara Jetty. In six kms. from Rangat, there is a beautiful beach called Amkunj beach with a total length of about 1½ kms. and width of 40 mts. This beach is surrounded by tropical rain forest. One more beach near the Rangat is Chatbut Bay which has a turtle nesting ground. All turtles come to this beach and hatch their eggs 70-150 at a stretch, during full moon days. This is really worth seeing.

Tourists can stay in the guest house owned by the APWD, under the control of Executive Engineer, Rangat, with the prior permission of the Chief Engineer, Port Blair. A cook is attached with the guest house. He will provide all Indian dishes at normal rate on order. Recently, a private lodge came in existence where, too, tourists can stay at reasonable tariff. There are some other good hotels (only eating places) near the bus stand. They, too, provide good food at reasonable rates. Tourists have to place an order in advance in case of any special items they want, like prawn fry, costly fish like surmai, chicken items, etc.

Barren Island : Barren Island is situated at a distance of 135 kms by sea. It is an uninhabited island. The only active volcano in India is in this Island named 'Barren Island Volcano'. It errupted twice in the recent past, once in 1991 and again in 1994-95 after 177 years. This Island, about three kms. in diameter, has a big crater of volcano, which raises abruptly from the sea, about half kms. from the shore and is about 150 fathoms deep. At present, the volcano is again dormant. Tourists cannot go to this island. However, with the permission of the Andaman & Nicobar Administration, one can go here for some academic purpose.

Mayabunder : It is situated in the northern most part of Middle Andaman. The distance between Port Blair and Mayabunder is about 240 kms. and Mayabunder and Rangat is about 70 kms. by road. The sea distance betwen Port Blair and Mayabunder is 135 kms. Mayabunder is the administrative headquarters for the Middle Andaman and North Andaman. The total population of Mayabunder is 21,570 mainly rural, as per 1991 census. The population of Mayabunder consists of Tamilians, Malayalis, Bengalis and a few Burmese settlers, with a distinct culture. There are 71 census villages in the

Mayabunder. Comparatively the Mayabunder, being headquaters, has better infrastuctural facilities like hospitals, provision of water, electricity, communications, internal transport, etc. Mayabunder has a number of islands and beaches surrounding it. Of these beaches, a charming beach called Karmatang beach is situated at a distance of 12 kms. from Mayabunder bus terminus. This is an excellent beach for snorkling, diving, and swimming. This beach is very famous for turtle nesting like Chutbut Bay in Rangat. Tourists can go and see, during full moon days, hatching of turtles which is very interesting. Mayabunder has excellent scenic beauty, and sunrise and sunset are really worth seeing. The tourists can reach Mayabunder by road or by boat. The boat journey takes 12 hours whereas the bus journey takes seven to eight hours. Tourists can enjoy the natural beauty of the creeks, mangrove forests, open sea fishes, dances of dolphins, flying fishes etc, while going by boat. If they choose road transport, they can enjoy the real natural forest beauty when the buses go by crossing the reserved forests area where the aborigins Jarawas are living. The vehicle ferry will help the buses to cross a big creek in two places, one is Middle Strait Jetty and the other one Uttara Jetty. While crossing the forest area the beauty of the forests draw the attention of the tourists. In Mayabunder, there is a beautiful government guest house under the control of APWD, A & N Administration. Four cooks are attached with the guest houses and they provide, on order, all types of Indian food at comparatively cheaper rates. They move with the tourists , really by treating them, as if the tourists were their guests. From Mayabunder guest house, the view particularly at the time of sunrise and moonrise is very fascinating. The tourists can stay in the guest house by taking prior permission from the Chief Engineer, APWD, Port Blair.

Diglipur : Diglipur is in the North Andaman. It is an inhabited island. The sea distance between Diglipur and Port Blair is 185 kms. and Mayabunder and Diglipur is 28 kms. The total population of these islands is 23,734 mainly rural as per 1991 census. The settlers of this island are

Bengalis, Malayalis, Tamilians and Telugus. The main occupation of the population is cultivation of paddy, vegetable and fruits. Diglipur island is observed as the "Granary of A & N Islands" and it is famous for oranges. Saddle peak, the highest point in Andaman & Nicobar Islands (732 mtrs), is near this Island. Kalipur sandy beach has been developed as a tourist complex. Tourists can reach the island by boat directly from Port Blair or from Aerial Bay or from Mayabunder. Otherwise, tourists can go upto Mayabunder by bus, and from Mayabunder to Kalighat village by a small boat by crossing, Mayabunder Kalighat creek which is the longest one. From Kalighat to Diglipur they can go by bus. Tourists can see crocodiles while crossing the creek. Tourists can stay in the Goverment guest house with the prior permission of the Chief Engineer, APWD, Port Blair.

5

TOURISM FACILITIES

The growth and development of tourism depends upon two important factors. They are the attractions and facilities. Tourism attractions have already been discussed in the previous chapter. Generally the availability and quality of facilities are considerably responsible for the duration of the stay of a tourist and also indirectly in promoting further attractions for the tourist centre.This is very much particular of the places like A & N Islands. Any tourist who comes to a destination, would like to know the different available facilities existing there. Then he/she would like to have comfortable facilities at most economical cost. Some tourists, before starting their journey, would plan and try to confirm about the various facilities available at the place or destination. If the travel is due to an invitation from his friends/relatives, or he is guided by a travel agent, or tour operator, he need not worry for the facilities since it becomes their responsibility to provide the same. As first impression is the best impression, the tourist facilities are counted for the better impression. Whatever be the level of richness of tourist attractions, if a destination fails to provide the tourist facilities, the tourists will not be attracted and will be dissatisfied. A satisfied tourist is the best advertiser and a dissatisfied tourist is the worst turndown friend. Hence the tourism facilities available in the A & N Islands to the tourists are highlighted in this chapter.

A & N Islands have a number of tourist facilites which are grouped into the following three catagories :

I. Basic Tourism Facilities
II. Supporting Tourism Facilties
III. Other Tourism Facilties.

The basic tourism facilties are further divided into Information Centres, Entry facilities, Transport, Communication, Places of Stay (accommodation) and Food, etc. The supporting facilities include Travel agents/Tour operators, Tourist Guides and Taxi Operators, etc. The other facilities are Shopping Health service, Photography , Banking service, Cinema, Swimming Pool, Clubs, etc. Of them, basic facilities are most important for the development of tourism. Without basic facilties, tourism industry cannot be developed. If the basic facilties are available, the industry is assured of the fundamental needs of its growth.

BASIC FACILITIES

Information Centres : Information constitutes the most important part in the package of tourism facilities offered to the tourists. This is the prime facility without which the tourists will not get even the first idea about the place, attractions, etc. Generally, tourists before coming to these far flung Islands, would wish to collect particulars and information regarding the places to see, best season to travel and visit, air tickets, ship tickets, fares, accommodation facilities available, tour operators, items to purchase, how long one can stay, accommodation tariff, procedure to get permission, immigration formalities, etc. Of the whole information some is to be collected before they come to these Islands on the mainland itself and the rest they can get after reaching these Islands i.e. in Port Blair. A & N Administration has provided this facility through its own offices both on the mainland and the Islands. Tourism Offices of the government of India and the private travel and tour agents/operators at the different parts of our country share the responsibility of providing necessary information to the tourists. For the purpose of information to the tourists, the following addresses are given from where all the tourists, both the domestic and foreign, can obtain the particulars and information.

New Delhi

1. The Resident Commissioner,
   A&N Administration,
   Andaman & Nicobar Bhavan, Plot No.12
   Chanakyapuri, Near Chanakya Cinema
   New Delhi-110 021
   Phone : (011) 6871443
   Fax : (011)3783642

Chennai

1. Andaman House, North Main Road Ext.,
   Anna Nagar West Ext., Padi Village
   Chennai - 600 101
   Phone (044) 6259255

Calcutta

1. Chief Liaison Officer,
   A&N Administration.
   3-A Auckland Place,Calcutta-700 017
   Phone (033) 24755084
   Fax: (033) 24755084

2. Sagar Travels.

A & N Islands(Port Blair)

1. Directorate of Tourism
   A & N Administration
   Port Blair - 744 101
   Phone 30933,32488,& 32747.

2. Tourist Information Centre
   Airport, Lamba Line

Inside the Campus
Port Blair
(On all flight days), Phone 32414.

3. Tourist Information Centre
Andaman Teal House
Delanipur, Port Blair
Phone 32642.

4. Govt.of India Tourist Office.
89, Junglighat, Main Road,
Port Blair-744 103
Phone 33006.

5. Govt.of India Tourist Information Counter,
Lamba Line Airport,
Inside the Campus
(On all flight days except Sundays)

6. All Tour Operators (Addresses are given under the Travel & Tour Operators- sub heading.)

Entry/Permission : At the time of interview and collection of questionaires from the tourists, the most interesting question from them was whether they could go to tribal areas and see them. The tourists repeatedly say that they have read somewhere that they can go freely and see, meet and talk with all the tribals, as seen in the photos of tribals standing with non-tribals. Again, they add that they have been told that they can visit all places, Islands etc., without any restriction. After coming to Port Blair, they get upset and are disappointed when they come to know that they have to take permission to go to tribal areas. This disappointment, frustration etc., are due to the lack of information about the rules and regulations of entry, permission etc. Therefore, it is necessary to clear the misrepresentation, made by some writers without having properly studied the rules and regulations related to the visit of these areas so that no tourist feels misled about these Islands. No doubt, the tourism industry has grown in these Islands but at the same time, due to some technical and defence reasons, all the Islands under this territory are not open to tourists including Indian tourists. For the purpose of development of tourism these islands are divided into three from the tourism point of view, namely:

1. Tribal Area
2. Non Tribal Areas Open to Foreign Tourists
3. Non Tribal Areas Open to Indian Tourists.

Tribal Areas : A clear picture of the tribals and their areas of living have already been given in Chapter III .These are prohibited areas for tourists. Areas where the tribals Jarawa and Sentinelese are living are completely prohibited for all tourists including Indian tourists. The places/Islands where Onges, Great Andamanese and Nicobar tribals are living are also restricted areas. However, only Indian tourists are granted permission by the A & N Administration to visit these restricted areas and no foreign tourist is granted permission to visit any tribal areas.

Non-Tribal Areas Open to Foreign Tourists : During the early years, the foreigners were not allowed to go, visit and stay beyond the municipal limits of Port Blair. Then the government allowed the foreigners to visit Jolly Bouy Islands, Redskin Islands, Wandoor National Park, Cinque Islands during the day time only. But now besides the above places/Islands, the following places/areas/Islands are also declared open by the government to the foreign tourists :

1. Havelock Island in South Andaman
2. Mount Hariet in South Andaman
3. Neil Island in South Andaman
4. Rangat in Middle Andaman
5. Mayabunder in Middle Andaman
6. Long Islands in Middle Andaman and
7. Diglipur Islands in North Andaman.

Foreign tourists can stay in these Islands (permitted areas) initially for a period of 30 days. However, with the permission of the government of India the foreign tourists can stay for more than 30 days also. For the purpose of the 30 days' stay, they require a permit which is to be (but can be easily) obtained from the immigration authorities on arrival at Port Blair either at the airport or at the harbour. The foreign tourists can also obtain the permit from the Indian Embassy of their respective country itself or from any of the four Foreign Regional Registrar Offices (FRRO) situated in Chennai, Calcutta, Mumbai and Delhi. The mailing addresses are as follows:

1. **Chennai**
   The Officer Incharge
   Foreign Regional Registrar Office(FRRO)
   9, Village Road
   Chennai. Phone: (044) 478210.
2. **Calcutta**
   The Officer Incharge
   FRRO, 237, A.J.Bose Road
   Calcutta
   Phone: (033) 443301.

3. **Mumbai**
   The Officer Incharge
   FRRO, Special Branch II Annexe 2,
   Office of the Commissioner of Police,
   Dadabhoy Naroji Road,
   Mumbai
   Phone (022) 268111.

4. **Delhi**
   The Officer Incharge
   FRRO,
   Ist Floor, Hans Bhawan,
   Tilak Bridge.
   Delhi
   Phone (011) 272790.

Do's and Don'ts : All tourists are expected that they should not damage the tourism resources particularly the marine life resources. For that purpose, the A&N Administration has given the following guidelines in the form of Do's and Don'ts.

Do's *

Treat the Park with respect as it is a sanctum sanctorum of our precious natural heritage.

* Make use of the services of tourist guides.
* Learn more about coral reefs, other marine life and tropical forests. This will make your visit more enjoyable.
* Help us to keep the Park clean. Always take back litter.
* Take care of the reef, not just for yourself but for all who follow.
* Give your valuable comments and observations for ensuring better park management.

Don'ts

* Do not enter the Park without permit.
* Do not collect, destroy or remove any living or dead animal/plant.
* Do not collect dead coral or break live coral. Please do not stand on the coral reef while snorkelling.
* Do not take video or film without permit.

TRANSPORT

Tourism and transport are inter-related with each other. Tourism will improve if the transport facilities are good and the transport will improve if tourism is good and hence they are inseparable. "Tourism is about being elsewhere and a major component of any tourist activity must necessarily be an element of transportation". It is the end result of travel which makes the movement of the people from one place to another. Transport and communication are considered as an integral part of tourism. In the words of Robinson, "Transport has been at once a cause and an effect of growth of tourism. Improved transport facilities have stimulated tourism, the expansion of tourism has stimulated transport". The relationship between transport and tourism can be expressed as "The transport is to tourism what veins and arteries are to body system".

Majority of the tourists travel for pleasure and they want their journey to be comfortable, congenial and relaxed one. The tourists get their happiness, joy, relaxation, eagerness, awareness, pleasure and expectations fully if they travel by proper transport without any problem. Otherwise the tourist may get frustrated, dissatisfied and disappointed and he or they may be a dangerous factor to the tourism industry as a whole. So "comfortable and efficient transport facilities are the sin-qua-non of a tourism industry". "Better transport facility increases the volume of tourist attractions and vice- versa". Tourism in Andaman and Nicobar Islands is of a special type. Foreign tourists first have to come to Calcutta, Chennai or Vishakhapatnam. After reaching any one of the three cities they have to wait for a ship or a flight to Andaman and Nicobar Islands (Port Blair). After arriving at Port Blair tourists go to different places in Andaman and Nicobar Islands. The transport facilities available in or provided by A & N Islands are classified for the purpose the present work, into four categories namely :

1. Inter-country transport
2. Islands-mainland transport
3. Inter-Islands transport
4. Local road transport.

Inter-Country Transport : This is related to foreign tourists coming to these islands. The A&N Administration does not provide any transport facilities as regards the inter-country transport . However this system has now been greatly intensified by flights, more so by speed flights. Hence it is not discussed in the present work.

Islands-Mainland Transport : Under this category both airplanes and ships are utilised. This sector of the transport forms an integral part of the island tourism. Tourists, both Indian and foreign, come to these islands by means of flight and ships which constitute the only transport system between the Islands and the mainland of India. All the goods from cement to sugar, vegetables to salt are brought into these islands both by ships and flights more so by ships. Hence Island-Mainland transport consists of air and shipping services.

Shipping Service : At present there are four ships plying between mainland of India and A&N Islands. The names of these ships are :

1. M.V.Nicobar
2. M.V.Nancowry
3. M.V Harshwardhan and
4. M.V Akbar

These ships are operated between Port Blair-Chennai-Port Blair, Port Blair-Calcutta-Port Blair, and Port Blair Vishakhapatnam-Port Blair. Though no particular ship is permanently meant for a particular sector, M.V.Nancowry is generally plying on Port Blair-Chennai-Port Blair sector, M.V.Nicobar on Port Blair-Calcutta-Port Blair sector the other two ships are operated for all the three sectors depending upon the availability of other ships. They are sent to mainland at different periods for two-three months' duration for Annual Passenger Survey (APS) which is a statutory requirement of the four ships. Ships are also sent for repairs and maintenance besides APS. So the number of ships available for tourists and passengers, on an average, is minimum two and maximum is three. Ships are operated on Port Blair-Chennai-Port Blair sector for a minimum of four times and on Port Blair - Calcutta-Port Blair sector for a minimum of four times a month. The tourists, both the domestic and foreign, can get their reservation of tickets, shipping programes and other relevant information from the four cities, namely, Mumbai, Calcutta, Chennai and Vishakhapatnam. Normally, the shipping programs are made by the A&N Administration and sent to these places for the use of the tourists. The following addresses are useful for tourists, from where all information about shipping services can be collected/ obtained.

Mumbai

The Director/Dy.Director/Manager
Shipping Corporation of India Limited
Coastal Passenger Service division
Discovery of India Building
5th Floor, Nehru Centre
Annie Besant Road, Worli
Mumbai - 400018
Telephone No.(022)4931461

Calcutta

1. The Director/Dy.Director/Manager
   Shipping Corporation of India Limited
   Shipping House
   No.18 Strand Road
   Calcutta
   Telephone No.(033)284456
2. Chief Liaison Officer
   A & N Administration
   3-A Auckland Place
   Calcutta - 700017
   Telephone No. (033) 24755084
   Fax No. (033) 24755084.

Chennai

1. The Director/Dy.Director/Manager
   Shipping Corporation of India Ltd.
   Madras Port Trust
   Rajaji Salai
   Chennai

Telephone No.(044) 5231401
(044) 5131410

2. The Deputy Director of Shipping Services
A&N Administration
6 Rajaji Salai
Chennai
Telephone No.(044) 5220841
(044) 5226873

3. Dy. Resident Commissioner
A&N Administration
C.P.W.D Campus.
K.K.Nagar
Chennai - 600078
Telephone No.(044) 4844715
Fax No. (044) 4844715

4. Andaman House
North Main Road Ext.,
Anna Nagar West Ext.,
Padi Village
Chennai - 600101
Telephone No. (044) 6259295

Vishakhapatnam

M/S A.V.Bahanojirow and Garuda Pattabhiramayya & Co
Agent-Shipping Corporation of India Ltd.
Post Box No. 17
Vishakhapatnam

Information can also be collected directly from Port Blair over phone or by post or by fax or by telegram from the following addresses:-

1. The Directorate of Shipping Services
A & N Administration
Phoenix Bay Jetty

Port Blair - 744101
Telephone No. (03192) 32725
Telephone No. (03192) 32742

2. Shipping Corporation of India Ltd.
   Aberdeen Bazar
   Port Blair - 744101
   Telephone No. (03192) 32971

3. The Director
   Tourism Department
   A&N Administration
   Port Blair - 744101
   Telephone No. (03192) 30933
   32747
   32694
   Fax No. (03192) 30933
   32656
   30234

Procedure for Tickets : The tourists have to come to Chennai, Vishakhapatnam or Calcutta at least two days in advance, if they have talked to the concerned officials of the above addressed offices or reserved their tickets to otherwise at least five days in advance to contact the above offices or ticket issuing authority. The prescribed application form is to be filled up and two passport size photographs are also to be attached. The tickets are issued on first come first serve basis.The tourists are advised to contact the offices at least 15 days before by telegram/fax/post or telephone.

Ship Fare : The A&N Administration is the authority to fix the fare for all the Island-Mainland. Taking into account a lot of concessions, subsidies and incentives given to the departments/organisations operating shipping services, the fares are fixed. The present rates which are applicable to tourists are given in Table 5:1.

Table 5.1
Ship Fares Applicable to Tourists
w.e.f. 1.11.96

Class	M.V. Nicobar	M.V. Nancowry	M.V. Harshavardhan	M.V. Akbar
Delux	3450	3450	3450	3450
'A'Class Cabin	2852	2852	-	-
I Class Cabin	-	-	2852	2427
'B'Class Cabin	2243	2243	-	-
4&6 Berth Cabin	-	-	2243	-
II Class Cabin	-	-	1725	1440
'AC ' Ordinary Bunk	955	955	955	828

Source : Andaman Herald

Ship Journey : For all tourists the ship journey may be the first experience. This is to be really enjoyed .The best season for the ship journey is from October to mid December and from mid January to April end. During this period the sea remains calm. Sitting on the deck/terrace (Top floor of the ship-open space) with a glass of cold drink and a plate of Karam mixture, seeing the blue waters in a pleasant weather, gives really a happy and cheerful feeling. Sunrise and sunset are the marvellous sights which one should not miss watching. The dolphins and flying fishes are always visible and they show their presence by jumping up and down and flying. All such scenes can also be enjoyed sitting inside the cabin by keeping the window open. Films, thambola etc. are also arranged inside the ships. Medical, shopping, bar, canteen facilites are also provided on the ship. Some tourists/travellers may develop mild sea sickness which can be avoided. The travellers who feel a vomiting sensation should chew the lemon pickles. The travellers may carry the following eatables with them for full enjoyment .The quantity of eatables given in Table 5.2 is for one person for three days.

Table 5.2
Eatables to be carried during Ship Journey

Item	Qty for One Person
Avomine Tablets	3 Nos.
Lemon/Ginger/Mango Pickle	100 grams.
Bread	2 Pkts.
Jam	50 grams.
Heavy Karam Mixture	250 grams
Salt Biscuits	2 Pkts.
Lemon Fruit	3 Nos.
Orange or apple	3 Nos.

Source : Primary Data - Personal Experience

The information on the level of sea sickness during various months is given in Table 5.3. It is clear that the best season for tourism in these islands is from October 15 to May 15.

Duration of Journey : The ships are expected to reach the destination within 54 hrs.; however the ship journey takes three nights and two days or three days and two nights depending upon the weather conditions. If weather conditions are favorable the ship reaches the destination even before the scheduled time, otherwise it takes even more than five days. But during the tourists' season, the ships reach the destination on time.

Air Service : Next to the shipping service air service is considered to be second lifeline of these Islands. Though the air service is one of the means of travel, here in these Islands, it is considered essential for quick travel. Air transport service to these islands is provided by Indian Airlines and East West Airlines. It significantly contributes to the development of tourism in this lush green heaven. The air traffic to and from this Island is divided into four sectors namely:

1. Chennai-Port Blair – Calcutta
2. Calcutta-Port Blair-Chennai
3. Delhi-Bhubneswar-Port Blair-Delhi
4. Port Blair-Car Nicobar-Port Blair.

Table 5.3
Level of Sickness

Month	Level of Sea Sickness			
	More	Certainly	Slight	Not at all
January	-	-	-	✓
February	-	-	-	✓
March	-	-	-	✓
April	-	-	-	✓
May (upto 15th)	-	-	-	✓
May (upto 31st)	-	-	✓	-
June (upto 15th)	-	-	✓	-
June (upto 30th)	-	✓	-	-
July	✓	-	-	-
August	✓	-	-	-
September	✓	-	-	-
October (upto 15th)	-	✓	-	-
October (upto 30th)	-		-	✓
November	-	-	-	✓
December (upto 20th)	-	-	✓	-
December (upto 31st)	-	-	-	✓

Source:- Own Experience - Primary Data.

For all these sectors Indian Airlines has been providing a fairly good service to tourists to and from this territory. Due to some technical problems the Indian Airlines could not operate its service in 3&4 sectors. In 1995, East West Airlines introduced its air service operation to Port Blair -Chennai. But due to some unknown problem the operation of the service has been stopped temporarily. So, at present only Indian Airlines is operating its services through Boeing 737 flights on only two sectors namely Chennai-Port Blair- Calcutta and Calcutta-Port Blair-Madras. The particulars of flight days time of arrival and departure are given in Tables 5.4 and 5.5. Though the air journey is quick and pleasant, it is

Table 5.4
Particulars of Flights To Port Blair

S.No	Particular	From Chennai	From Calcutta
1.	Flight Number	IC 549	IC 285
2.	Operating Days	Tuesday Thursday Saturday	Monday Wednesday Friday
3.	Departure Time	6.15 am	5.30 am
4.	Arrival Time	8.20 am	7.30 am
5.	Ticket Fare		
	For Full (Rs)	5,310.00	5,250.00
	For Half (Rs.)	2,695.00	2,660.00
	For Student(Rs)	3,035.00	3,000.00
	For Infant (No seat)	460.00	455.00
6.	Excess Baggage Per kg. over 20 kg.	50.10	49.55

Source: Indian Airlines- Port Blair.

Table 5.5
Particulars of Flights

			From Port Blair
S.No	Particulars	To Chennai	To Calcutta
1.	Flight Number	IC 550	IC 286
2.	Operating Days	Monday Wednesday Friday	Tuesday Thursday Saturday
3.	Departure Time	8.10 am	9.00 am
4.	Arrival Time	10.15 am	11.00 am
5.	Ticket Fare for Full	5310.00	5250.00
	For Half (Rs)	2695.00	2660.00
	For Student	3035.00	3000.00
	For Infant (No seat)	460.00	455.00
6.	Excess Baggage per kg over 20 kg.	50.10	49.55

Source: Indian Airlines, Port Blair.

comparatively expensive. But people of this territory use the air service as a means to go to the mainland and return on urgent occasions. The duration of journey is about two hrs. The tourists can approach any Indian Airlines office for reservation, information and tickets. All Boeing flight service operations have been taken over by Alliance Ltd. which is a subsidiary company of Indian Airlines from 26.11.96. Except the change in name, no other change in operation has taken place.

Inter Island Transport : Inter-Island transport system is the nervous system of the body i.e. A&N Islands. The transport system connects all the inhabited islands of this territory as these islands are located at a considerable distance from one another. All produces and products of the islands are distributed among them through the network system of Inter-island transport. It promotes cultural, social, trade, commerce and industrial activities in this territory. Inter-Island tourism depends highly on this transport system. This network consists of two kinds of transport namely water transport and road transport.

Inter-Island Waterways .: The capital of A&N Islands, Port Blair is connected with other Islands through the water and road transport. The Inter-Island water transport is further divided into ship service and foreshore ferry service. Four passenger-cum-cargo ships namely, M.V.Sentinel, M.V.Chowra, T.S.S.Yerawa, and M.V.Derring are plying between the Islands. In fact the four ships are the backbone of Inter-Island tranpsort. These ships are manned and maintained by the Shipping Corporation of India under the operational control of Director of Shipping Services. These ships may ply from Port Blair to Diglipur in north and Campbell Bay in south. A round voyage from Port Blair to Diglipur takes three days and to Campbell Bay seven days. While making voyage these vessels touch the different islands namely Hutbay, Nancowry, Car Nicobar, Rangat, Mayabunder, Neil, Havelock etc.

Foreshore Ferry Service: This type of Inter-Island water service is operated by the A&N Administration between Port Blair and nearby Islands and ports like Neil, Havelock, Rangat, Kadamtala, Baratang, etc. Generally small vessels are utilised for this service. Since these vessels are smaller in size, the foreshore ferry service heavily depends on weather condition. There are 49 vessels (small size) which are being used in the foreshore service as passenger cum cargo, V.I.P. special, only cargo, etc. The distance by sea between important places of A&N Islands in nautical miles and equivalent kms. is given in Table 5.6. The passenger tariff/fare for the Inter-Island water transport for different places/points is given in Table 5.7.

Table 5.6
Distance by Sea between Important Places

From	To	Distance	Distance
Port Blair	Diglipur	100	183
	Mayabunder	85	155
	Rangat	50	92
	LongIsland	46	84
	Havelock	21	38
	Oral Katcha	35	64
	Wrefter	27	49
	Long Island(via Oral Katcha)	45	82
	Mayabunder via Havelock	75	137
	Mayabunder via Long Island	74	135
	Little Andaman	66	121
	Car Nicobar	150	274
	Narcondum	140	256
	Nancowry	235	429
	Nancowry via Car Nicobar	230	420
	Barren Island	75	137
	Neil Island	20	37
	Baratang	35	64
	Kadamtala	50	92
	(Uttara Jetty)East Island	120	219
	Katchal	228	416
	Campbell Bay	294	537

Contd...

	South Bay (Great Nicobar)	300	548
Car Nicoabr	Chowra	55	100
	Teressa	45	82
	Katchal	80	146
	Nancowry	82	150
	Campbell Bay	155	283
Nancowry	WB Katchal	50	91
	Kandul	20	37
	Pulomilo	15	27
Narcondum	East Island	75	137
	Diglipur	7	13
	Mayabunder	85	155
	North Sentinel	198	361
	Hut Bay	200	365
Terressa	Nancowry	30	55
Campbell Bay	Kondul	30	55
Bareen Island	Mayabunder	66	121
	Long Island	55	100
	Nancowry	255	465
Kondul	Pulomilo	20	37

Source:- Basic Statistics, A&N Administration, Port Blair.

Table 5.7
Passenger Tariff for Inter-Islands/Foreshore Services (in Rs.)

Station From	To	Delux Cabin	Ordinary Cabin	Special Bunk	Deck
A. Southern Group of Islands					
1. Port Blair	Hut Bay	114.00	56.00	25.00	14.00
	Car Nicobar	226.00	113.00	49.00	29.00
	Katchal	347.00	174.00	74.00	43.00
	Nancowry	347.00	174.00	74.00	43.00
	Campbell Bay	460.00	230.00	103.00	64.00
2. Hut Bay	Car Nicobar	113.00	57.00	24.00	17.00
	Nancowry	258.00	130.00	57.00	38.00
	Campbell Bay	372.00	186.00	85.00	55.00

Contd...

3.	Car Nicobar	Teressa	106.00	53.00	24.00	14.00
		Katchal	151.00	75.00	32.00	19.00
		Nancowry	146.00	73.00	32.00	20.00
		Campbell Bay	258.00	129.00	61.00	41.00
4.	Nancowry	Pillomillow	73.00	36.00	17.00	12.00
5.	Nancowry	Campbell Bay	113.00	57.00	29.00	20.00
6.	Pillomillow	Kondul	41.00	20.00	12.00	8.00
7.	Katchal	Nancowry	32.00	16.00	9.00	5.00
8.	Teressa	Katchal	63.00	34.00	15.00	9.00
9.	Nancowry	Terressa	100.00	50.00	23.00	13.00
		Chowra	106.00	53.00	24.00	14.00
		Kondul	113.00	57.00	29.00	20.00
10.	Nancowry	Dering	15.00	9.00	4.00	3.00
		Pillowmillo	68.00	34.00	15.00	9.00
B.	**Middle and Northern Group of Islands**					
11.	Port Blair	Baratang		24.00		6.00
		Kadamtala		36.00		10.00
		Long Island		40.00		10.00
		Strait Island		40.00		10.00
		Rangat Bay		48.00	22.00	13.00
		Neil Island		20.00	10.00	6.00
12.	Port Blair	Havelock		24.00	11.00	6.00
		Mayabunder	157.00	79.00	36.00	20.00
		Diglipur	205.00	102.00	47.00	27.00
13.	Baratank	Kadamtala		13.00		3.00
		Long Island		16.00		5.00
14.	Baratang	Rangat		28.00		8.00
15.	Kadamtala	Long Island		4.00		2.00
16.	Kadamtala	Rangat Bay		18.00		5.00
17.	Long Island	Rangat Bay		14.00	6.00	4.00
		Mayabunder		40.00	18.00	10.00
		Diglipur		62.00	29.00	17.00
18.	Rangat Bay	Mayabunder		33.00	15.00	9.00
		Diglipur		57.00	26.00	15.00
19.	Neil Island	Havelock	18.00	8.00	5.00	
20.	Mayabunder	Diglipur	48.00	24.00	11.00	10.00

Contd...

21. Neil Island	Long Island	17.00	19.00	11.00	
	Rangat Bay		23.00	21.00	12.00
	Mayabunder		75.00	34.00	19.00
	Diglipur		98.00	44.00	25.00
22. Havelock	Neil Island		32.00	15.00	8.00
	Rangat Bay		44.00	20.00	10.00
	Mayabunder		71.00	32.00	19.00
	Diglipur		94.00	43.00	24.00

Note - Free baggage allowance - 40 Kg cabin, 30 kg for bunk class 25 kg for Deck class, excess baggage is as per cargo freight rates.

Source :- Basic Statistics, A&N Administration, Port Blair.

Road Transport : The roads are the main means of travel in a particular island. Rail transport is totally absent in these islands and hence road transport is very important for both long and short distances. Road transport in each Island of this territory has brought a significant change in the tourism industry and other allied activities. Road transport provides opportunity to tourists to enjoy the places, forests, nallahs etc., from close quarters. If one travels from Port Blair to Mayabunder by ship, it will take 12 hours. Distance by road between the places is give in Table 5.8.

Table 5.8
Distance by Road from Port Blair Bus Terminus

From	To	Distance (in kms)
Port Blair Bus Terminus	Chatham	5
	Haddo Jetty	5
	Buniyada Bad	5
	Dairy Farm	5
	Shadipur	5
	Dolly Gunj	10
	Bird Line	12
	School Line	6
	Garacharma	10

Teylarebad	12
Calicut	14
Sippighat	14
Minnie Bay	10
Pema Tekkri	16
Chouldhari	20
Burma Nala	20
Manjeri	24
Port Mout	24
Madhuban	75
Carbynscove	7
Mount Harriet	55
Namunaghar	30
Chidia Toppu	28
Wandoor	30
Tirur	36
Dandas Point	32
Ferrargunj	34
Wimberlygunj	42
Jirkatang	64
Bambooflat Jetty	46
Middle Strait	100
Rangat	170
Mayabunder	240

Source : Basic Statistics, A & N Administration.

Each means of transport in these islands has its own significant role in the tourism industry. Though the length of roads is less in these islands the longest road called Andaman Trunk Road (ATR) connects a number of villages, places of tourist interest. The work is continuing on constructing the Andaman Trunk Road. The length of Andaman Trunk Road at present is 289 kms.

The road transport system is being organised by motor transport department under the control of Director of Transport. Though the road passenger service was solely

organised by State Transport Service (STS), the A&N Administration has granted permission to private bus owners to run their buses for the passenger service. The A&N Administration is operating five express buses namely Express A, Express B, Express C, Express D and Express E on the ATR route. The buses start from Port Blair at 5.00 a.m., 5.30 a.m, 6.00 a.m. 6.30 am and 11.00 a.m and reach Mayabunder in nine hours and Rangat in seven hours (approximately). Besides these five buses, recently the two private luxury buses owned by TCI and private individuals are in operation over ATR route. The number of private buses and government buses plying on the roads of A&N Islands has been increasing. The tourism department organises sight seeing programe on road by their buses and vans. Likewise some private lodge owners also have their own buses and help the tourists who stay in their lodges/hotels. Some tourists, invited by their friends and relatives use scooters, motorcycles or even cars of their friends for sight seeing. Recently two entrepreneurs have started a new facility for the tourists of these Islands, of giving scooter, scooty, motrocycle, T.V.S.50, M-80 etc. on hire basis. The addresses of these entrepreneurs are given for the purpose of information to the tourists.

1. T.S.Guruswamy & Sons
   Aberdeen Bazar
   Port Blair.
   Phone- 33185.

2. Gurupreeth Singh
   Aberdeen Bazar
   Port Blair
   Phone:-

The tariff for such vehicles is given in Table 5.9.

Table 5.9
Hire Tariff for Two Wheelers

(Without fuel)

S.No	Vehicle	Full Day (Rs.)	Half Day (Rs.)
1.	Motor Bikes	120.00	75.00
2.	Scooter	120.00	75.00
3.	Mopeds	90.00	75.00

Sources : T.S Guruswamy & Sons, Aberdeen Bazar Port Blair as on 1.1.96.

Communication

A&N Islands are situated at a far away distance separated by thick blue water of the Bay of Bengal. Once the passenger/ tourist reaches the Island, naturally he/she is cut off from mainland. The situation was bad during 1960s, 70s and even upto mid of 80s. The A&N Islands are now provided with communication facilities though not fully to a satisfactory level. Particulars about the Islands, availability of accommodation air tickets, ship tickets etc., should be known to tourists so as to enable them to give a shape to their programmes and plans. After coming to these Islands, messages to and from his own house, relatives and friends on the mainland or foreign countries are very important so that they can enjoy the beauty of this lush green sunny paradise without any worries.The importance of communication is in no way less than the importance of transport. In A&N Islands, the Port Blair city has a well developed network of modern means of communication system like speed post, telegram, telephone, STD/ISD facility, Fax, Teleprinter, wireless.

The Port Blair city has one Head Post Office, one Head Telegraphic Office and one Telephone Exchange. The other places and islands have post offices with telegram booking facilities. The postal facility in these islands are slowly increasing.Though the facility is not fully available to the

Andaman and Nicobar Islands
Inter Island Wireless Communication Channel

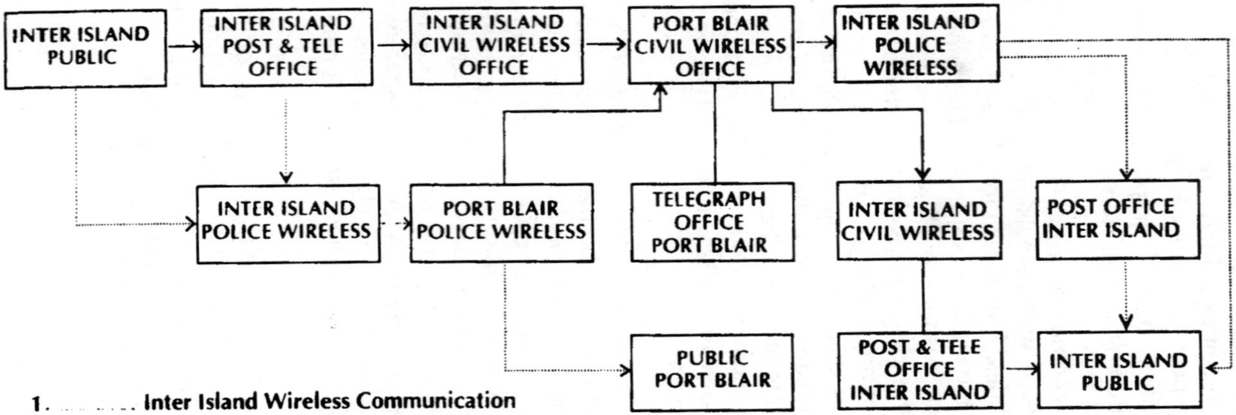

1. .... Inter Island Wireless Communication
2. .... The channel where there is no civil wireless.

Fig. 5.1

interior islands, the main Inter Islands have full communication facilities which are useful to all tourists. There are 32 sub-post offices, 64 branch post offices besides one head post office, one telegraphic office and telephone exchanges functioning in this territory.

Besides the telecommunication facilities, the A&N Islands have been provided with Television (Doordarshan) and All India Radio facilities. Port Blair Doordarshan and Port Blair All India Radio, having their studios at Delanipur (two kms from the Port Blair bus terminus), are an excellent means of communicating the ideas to the most interior parts where no other means of communication are possible. Moreover, the cable T.V operators share the social responsibility of providing communication means, thereby the people of these Islands enjoy different satellite T.V's Programmes. Almost all the hotels and other accommodations have the inter-com facilities in each room. However, only a few hotels have telephone facility in each room.

Four important dailies namely, *Daily Telegraph* in English, *Dweep Samachar* in Hindi, published by Andaman & Nicobar Administration and *Andaman Herald* in English and *Andaman Tamizhan* in Tamil published by a private person are from Port Blair city. Sunday editions are very useful to the tourists.Thirteen weekly papers are published in three languages. Strictly speaking, they are not weekly magazines, they are also like newspapers. As for magazines, sixteen issues are published in the city in eight languages. Particulars about the newspapers, weeklies etc., are given in Table 5.10.

Here in this territory the city telegraphic office has the facility of public call office (PCO). No post office is having this facility. However, many places in the city, main places of regions have the STD, ISD/PCO facilities, run by the educated unemployed persons.

Table : 5.10
Newspapers Published In Andaman And Nicobar Islands

Sl.No.	Name	Language
A. Daily		
1.	The Daily Telegraph	English
2.	Andaman Herald	English
3.	Dweep Samachar	Hindi
B. Weekly		
1.	Andaman Express	English
2.	Andaman Wave	English
3.	Andaman Sentinel	English
4.	Andaman Time	English
5.	Press Trust of India	English
6.	The Paravattum	English
7.	Light of Andaman	English
8.	A&N Tamil Marusu	English
9.	Dweep Manthon	Hindi
10.	Andaman Cheithi	Tamil
11.	Thee Paravattum	Tamil
12.	Andaman Tamilian	Tamil
13.	Andaman Thendral	Tamil
C. Fortnightly		
1.	Andaman Voice	English
2.	Deepon Ki Awaz	English
3.	Andaman Today	English
4.	Dweep Jan Jagrithi	English
5.	Andaman Sabdam	English
6.	Dweep Bani	Bengali
7.	Andaman Ki Lahar	Hindi
8.	Andaman Yugam	Malayalam
9.	Deep Maranu	Tamil
10.	Theevu Tamil Osai	Tamil
11.	A&N Congress Kural	Tamil

Contd...

D. Quarterly	
1. Jazeera	Urdu
E. Monthly	
1. Andaman Prabhatham	English
2. Dweep Katha	Hindi
3. Swastika	Bengali
4. Andaman Jagriti	Telugu

Source : Basic Statistics.

Accommodation

It is normal for a tourist to think about the food and lodging available at the place of destination. If the accommodation facility is not available, the tourists may be frustrated. As a tourist is quite new to the place of destination and he may not have any known person to the extent of seeking financial help at the tourist palce, he expects safe accommodation at a nominal tariff in accessible area. Many tourist places of stay etc. now having in the form of multi-storeyed buildings in Port Blair city. Hence the accommodation plays a vital role in the promotion of tourism in these Marigold Islands. The present situation regarding the accommodation is somewhat satisfactory at present. The available accommodation facility in A&N Islands is divided into, for the purpose of this present work, four types namely:

1. Govt. accommodation run by the Tourism Department
2. Semi-Govt. accommodation run by the ANIIDCO
3. Municipal Council accommodation run by the Municipal Council
4. Private accommodation

Government Accomodation : Particulars of government accommodation - name, address, tariff etc. for domestic tourists and foreign tourists are given in Table 5.11.

Table 5.11
Particulars of Govt. Accommodation (Tariff per day)

S.No.	Name & Address	Room For	Domestic Tourists A/C	Domestic Tourists Non-A/C	For Foreign Tourists A/C	For Foreign Tourists Non-AC
1.	Andaman Teal House, Delanipur	DB	300	200	(US$20) 600	(US$13) 400
2.	Hornbill Nest, Carbyn's Cove	DB	-	200	-	(US$13) 400
		FB	-	250	-	(US$16) 500
		SB	-	300	-	(US$20) 600
3.	New Guest House, Mohanpura	DB	-	150	-	(US$10) 300
4.	Sainik Vishram Ghar Haddo	DB	-	150	-	(US$10) 300
		SB	-	30*	-	(US$2) 60*
5.	Dolphine Yatri Niwas, Havelock	DB	400	200	(US$26) 800	(US$13) 400
6.	Hawabill Nest, Neil Island	DB	400	300	(US$26) 800	(US$20) 600
		FB	-	75	-	(US$5) 150
7.	Hawksbill Nest, Rangat	DB	400	250	(US$26) 800	(US$16) 500
		FB	-	75*	-*	(US$5) 150

Source :- Tourism Department Port Blair

Note :- * Per Bed DB- Double Beds SB -Six Beds FB- Four Beds.

For reservation in these accommodations, the tourists have to contact the following address.

The Director of Tourism
Andaman and Nicobar Administration
Department of Tourism
Port Blair - 744101
Telephone No. (03192) 32747, 30933, 32694
Fax No. (03192) 30933, 32656, 30234

Semi-Govt. Accommodation : The particulars of semi-Govt. accommodation - name, address, tariff for domestic tourists and foreign tourists are given in Table 5.12.

Table 5.12
Semi- Govt. Accommodation

Sl.No.	Name and Address	Room	A/C or Non A/C	Tariff
1.	Tourist Home Haddo Tel.20380	DB	A/C	500.00
2.	Magapode Nest Haddo Tel.20380	DB	A/C	500.00
3.	Nicobarese Cottage Haddo Tel:20207	DB	A/C	800.00

Source :- ANIIDCO, Port Blair, A&N Islands, DB-Double Bed

For the reservation purpose in these accommodation the tourists have to contact the following address,

The General Manager,
A&N Islands Integrated Development,
Corporation Ltd; (ANIIDCO),
New Marine Dry Docks,
Port Blair 744101,
Telephone No- (03192) 32076, 33650, 32098, 32380

Municipal Accommodation : The particulars of municipal accommodation- name, address, tariff for domestic tourist and foreign tourists are given in Table 5.13.

Table 5.13
Municipal Council Accommodation

Sl.No.	Name and Address	Room	A/C or Non A/C	Tariff
1.	New Municipal Guest House Aberdeen Bazar	DB	Non A/C	80.00
		TB	Non A/C	75.00
2.	Old Municipal Guest House Aberdeen Bazar	DB	Non A/C	20.00
		DMY	Non A/C	5.00
3.	Municipal Guest House Delanipur	-	Non A/C	25.00

Source:- Municipal Council, Port Blair
Note : DB-Double Beds, TB-Triple Beds, DMY-Dormitory.

For the reservation purpose in these accommodations the tourists have to contact the following address.

The Secretary Municipal Council
Aberdeen Bazar 744101
Telephone No. (03192) 32696

Private Accommodation : Paticulars of private accommodation - names, address, tariff for domestic tourists and foreign tourists are given in Table 5.14.

Table 5.14
Private Sector Accommodation

Sl. No.	Name & Address	Room	Tariff for Single	Tariff for Double
1.	Hotel Bay Island, Welcome Group, Marine Hill	A/C	1,945.00	3,500.00
	Tel : 32881	Deluxe A/C	1,845.00	3,300.00
	Fax : 33389	Deluxe non-A/C	1,745.00	3,000.00

Contd...

	Sea Facing A/C	-	3,800.00	
	Deluxe A/C	-	3,600.00	
	Deluxe Non-A/C	-	3,300.00	
2.	Peerless Resort, Carbyn'sCove, Port Blair	A/C	11,800.00	2,000.00
	Tel. 33462-64	Cottage A/C	1,800.00	2,500.00
	Fax. 33462 (Off-season discount 32%)	Extra bed		300.00
3.	Sinclairs Bay View, South Point, Port Blair	A/C	900.00	1,200.00
	Tel. 32973 / 33159	A/C	750.00	1,000.00
4.	Hotel Shompen, Middle Point, Port Blair	Non A/C	350.00	-
	Tel. 32360 / 32452	A/C	600.00	-
		A/C Deluxe	750.00	-
5.	Hotel Abhishekh, Goal Ghar, Port Blair	A/C	350.00	450.00
	Tel. 33565	Non-A/C	200.00	250.00
6.	Hotel N.K. International, Seashore Road, Port Blair	A/C	250.00	300.00
	Tel. 33066	Non-A/C	150.00	200.00
7.	Hotel Shalimar, Delanipur, Port Blair	A/C	-	300.00
	Tel. 33953	Non-A/C	150.00	190.00
8.	Hotel Dhanalakshmi, Aberdeen Bazar, Port Blair	Non A/C	200.00	300.00
	Tel. 33953	A/C	400.00	500.00
9.	Hotel Kavita, Aberdeen Bazar, Port Blair Tel. 33742	Non A/C	60.00	100.00
10.	Ram Niwas Lodge, Phoniex Bay, Port Blair Tel. 33337	Non A/C	35.00	65.00
11.	Tourist Cottage, Babu Line, Port Blair Tel. 33033	Non A/C	25.00	50.00

Contd...

12.	Sampath Lodge, Aberdeen Bazar, Port Blair Tel. 33752	Non A/C	30.00	60.00
13.	Manohar Lodge, Port Blair	Non A/C	25.00	50.00
14.	Hotel Bengal K.P., Babu Lane Back Side, Port Blair Tel. 32964	Non A/C	60.00	120.00
15.	K.K.Guest House, Port Blair	Non A/C	30.00	55.00
16.	Modern Lodge, Port Blair	Non A/C	25.00	
17.	Ratan Lodge, Port Blair Tel. 33333	Non A/C	30.00	50.00
18.	Sagar Alok Lodge, Port Blair Tel. 33587	Non A/C	50.00	60.00
19.	Anand Lodge, Haddo, Port Blair Tel. 33252	Non A/C	40.00	70.00
20.	Jagannath Guest House, Phoniex Bay, Port Blair Tel. 33154	Non A/C	75.00	100.00
21.	Phoniex Lodge, Phoniex Bay, Port Blair Tel. 33832	Non A/C	25.00	50.00
22.	Youth Hostel, Opp. Netaji Stadium, Port Blair Tel. 32459	Non A/C	40.00	

For the reservation purpose in these accommodations the tourists have to contact the address mentioned in the Table itself. Some Govt. guest houses are run and maintained by the PWD, Forest Department, etc. The tourists can stay there with the prior permission of the head of the respective department. For the purpose of tourists the particulars of the guest houses are given in Table 5.15.

Table 5.15
Govt.Guest Houses in Andaman & Nicobar Islands

Type	Location	Tehsil
Maintained by APWD	Circuit House Haddo	Port Blair
Tourist Home	"	"
Megapode Nest	"	"
Nicobarese Cottage (2 Nos)	"	"
Guest House No. II	"	"
Teal House	Delanipur	"
Horn BillNest	Doodhline	"
Tourist Home	Marine Hill	"
Guest House	Carbyn's Cove	"
Guest House	Neil Island	"
Guest House	Ferrargunj	Ferrargunj
Guest House	Wrightmyo	"
Guest House	Rangat	Rangat
Inspection Banglow	Baratang	"
Guest House	Kadamtala	"
Inspection Banglow	Hutbay	Little Andaman
Resthouse	Betapur	Rangat
Guest house	Mayabunder	Mayabunder
Rest house	Kalighat	"
Rest house	Kishori Nagar	"
Rest house	Diglipur	Diglipur
Rest house	Aerial Bay	"
Guest house	Car Nicobar	Car Nicobar
Circuit house	"	"
Annexure (for class III staff)	Malacca	"
Guest house	Campbell Bay	Nancowrie
Yatri Niwas	"	"
Guest house	Kamorta	"
Guest house	Katchal	"
Guest house Mainted	South Andaman	Port Blair by Chidiyatapu
Nilam bur	Baratang	"
Wandoor	South Andaman	Ferrargunj
Mount Harriet	"	"
Long Island	Middle Andaman	Rangat

Elphinstone Harbour	"	"
Bakultala	"	"
Aerial Bay	North Andaman	Diglipur

Besides the above accommodation facilities the regional associations also accommodate the visitors who are economically poor. Examples of such associations are Andaman Tamilar Sangam, Kerala Samajam, Maharashtra Mandal, Bengali Club, Hindi Sahitiya Kala Parishad etc., but these associations do not provide accommodation facility to the level of tourists' satisfaction.

Food

Food is one of the vital factors which determine the growth and development of tourism industry. Tourist destination should have the food facilities suitable for all tourists. What is suitable food to Bengalis may not be suitable to Tamil tourisis and Malayalam tourists and so is the case to the foreign tourist also. As for as food is concerned, all accommodations /hotels provide limited types of food. Indian style and foreign style are also available is some hotels like Annapurana and Ananda Sweet Stall and Restaurant situated at Aberdeen Bazar, Port Blair. The Dhanalakshmi restaurant is situated on the main road of Aberdeen Bazar, next to Dhanalakshmi. Kattaboman hotel, Thillai Restuarant, Milan hotel provide good vegetarian and non-vegetarian food. Good quality sweets, karams etc, can be purchased in Annapurana hotel, Ananda Sweet Stall and Restaurant and Vijayalakshmi Bhavan (near clock tower). Chinese food is available in Chinese Restaurant in Dignabad near Phonix Bay Jetty. Fried lobsters,fish, prawns are the special features of the restaurant.Tourists can make reservations. The restaurants and their addresses are given in Table 5.16.

SUPPORTING FACILITIES

Travel Agents Tour Operators : Generally the tourist attractions, entry facilities,transport facilities,

Table 5.16
Hotels and Restaurants in Port Blair

S.No.	Hotel/Restaurants/Cafeteria	Address
1.	Ananda Sweet Stall & Restaurant	Aberdeen Bazar
2.	Annapoorna Cafeteria	Aberdeen Bazar
3.	Darbar Hotel	Delanipur
4.	Delhi Cafeteria	Middle Point
5.	Kaja Peeja	Goalghar
6.	Kattapoman Hotel	Aberdeen Bazar
7.	Millan Hotel	Aberdeen Bazar
8.	New India Cafe	Phoniex Bay
9.	Quality fast food	Delanipur
10.	Royal Restaurant	Phoniex Bay

Source : Personal Collection.

accommodations etc. are the essential factors of the tourism industry and particularly in A&N Islands. But all these factors are independant and hence they are to be co-ordinated. So an intermediary agency is required to function as a co-ordinator who is termed as travel agent. Normally, these travel agents as tour operators have all transport facilities, information and guides etc. with them at different points in order to facilitate the tourists to reach the distination, place of interest etc. Their role in tourism industry is immense and they provide a number of attractive incentives to the tourists.The travel agents are divided into three categories namely, International Level Agents, National Level Agents and Regional Level Agents. As far as these islands are concerned, the travel agents are confined to the regional level. However, one or two agents have some connections with the Calcutta/Chennai Agents who are also regional agents. There are five travel agents or tour operators in these islands. Their addresses are as under:-

1. Sagar Tour & Travel Pvt. Ltd.,
   No.7, Krishna Building,
   Haddo,
   Port Blair.
2. Island Travels,
   Aberdeen Bazar
   Port Blair

3. Shompen Travels
   2, Middle Point
   Port Blair
   Ph: 32452, 33028 & 32644

4. Lokhnath Travels
   Lamba Line
   Port Blair

5. Baba Travels Pvt,Ltd
   Hindi Sahithya Kala Parished Building
   Port Blair
   Ph: 33222, 33139.

Of these five travel agents/tour operators, Sagar Travels Ltd., is approved by the Govt.of India . But as far as the services to the tourists the other unapproved travel agents/ tour operators too precisely function the same way as the approved travel agent. They organise the tours regularly as the tourism department is doing. The tour consists of 1. City Tour which covers Cellulor Jail, Mini Zoo, Cottage Emporium, Anthropological Museum, Samundrica, Chatham Saw Mill, Gandhi Park, Marina Park, etc. 2. Carbyn's Cove Tour which covers only Carbyn's Cove beach. 3. Chidiatoppu Tour which covers only Chidiyatoppu. 4. Excursion around South Andaman which includes Mahathma Gandhi National Marine Park, Wandoor, Red Skin, Jollybouy, Wandoor Beach etc. 5. Rose Islands Tour which covers only Rose Island. Besides these above tours, there is one more tour named Viper Horbour Cruise Tour which includes around 5 jetties. The particulars of City Tour,Excursion to Rangat & Mayabunder and the Excursion to and around South Andaman are given in Table 5.17, 5.18, 5.19.

Table 5.17
Particulars About Tour

Place/ Tour	Fare (in Rs.) Adult	Child	Timing
City Tour Bus	40/-	20/-	Tues -Sun 0830Hrs and 1200Hrs
Corbyn's Cove Bus	40/-	20/-	0830Hrs and 1700Hrs

Chidiya Tapu Bus	75/-	38/-	Tues-Sun 0900Hrs

OPERATED BY DIRECTORATE OF SHIPPING SERVICES FROM PHOENIX BAY JETTY (Tel - 32462, 32742)

Ross Island	Boat	13/-	4/-	Daily except Wed 0830,1000 & 1230Hrs
Viper/Harbour Cruise	Boat	20/-	7/-	Daily Except Wed 1500Hrs to 1700Hrs

Source :-Tourism Department-Port Blair.

Table : 5.18
Excursions Around South Andaman

Place	Route	Fare (in Rs.)		Timing
		Adult	Child	
MG Marine National Park, Wandoor	Bus	75/-	38/-	Tues-Sun-0830 hrs. Sun/State/Private Bus
Wandoor -Red Skin	Boat	50/-	25/-	Daily 1000 Hrs
Wandoor-Jolly Bouy	Boat	75/-	38/-	Daily 1000 Hrs
Wandoor Beach (Via Shippighat Agri.Farm & Rubber Plantation)	Bus	75/-	38/-	Tue-Sun at 0900Hrs

Source : Tourism Department A&N Administration, Port Blair.

Table 5.19
Excursion to Port Blair - Rangat - Mayabunder

Place	Route	Distance	Transport
Port Blair : Rangat	Bus	170 Kms	Road-Daily Journey Time 6 Hrs.
	Sea	90 Kms	Boat 4 times a week Journey Time 7 Hrs.
ROUTE: BY BUS			
1. **Port Blair**			
Middle Strait	Bus	100 Kms	Daily Bus Service
2. **Middle Strait**			
Nilamber Jetty	Ferry	1 Km	Daily

3. Nilamber Jetty			
Gandhi Ghat (for Baratang)	Bus	22 Kms	Every hour
4. Gandhi Ghat			
Kadamtala	Ferry	1 Km	Daily
5. Kadamtala			
Rangat	Bus	45Kms	Daily
Rangat	Bus	71 Kms	Daily
Mayabunder Boat	46 Kms	Thrice a week	
Note: Bus Fare upto Mayabunder :Excluding Ferry Charges = Rs. 47.00			
Mayabunder	Ferry & Bus	40 Kms	Daily
Diglipur	Boat	46 Kms	Twice a week.

Source: Tourism department, A&N Administration, Port Blair

Taxi/Car Operators : Due to the geographical location and structure of road, there is no three wheeler (Auto rickshaws) in these Islands. Only during the last month, some PMRY participants have brought three Auto rickshaws. Its performance is to be studied . But taxies are available to the tourists for the city travel.The taxi fare is given in the table 5.20. Getting motorbikes, scooters and mopeds for hire is the recent development in these Islands particularly in the city .M/S T.S.G & Sons, Aberdeen Bazar, Port Blair, Tel.Ph. 33185 provide two- wheeler facility on hire. Tariff/hire charges are given in Table 5.9.

Table 5.20
Taxi Fares in A & N Islands

S.No.	Distance/particulars	Rate (in Rs)
1.	For First 1½ kms	7.80
2.	For Subsequent every km	3.90
3.	For luggage charges upto 45 kgs	Nil
4.	For every additional 25 kgs or past thereof	2.50
5.	Waiting charges (per hour) (50 p.for every 3 min)	10.00
6.	Night Charges (10 PM to 5 AM)	25% Extra

For the group tourist cars are also available in the city without fuel or with fuel at negotiable rates. All car operators are in Port Blair city only. The addresses are:-

1. Island Travels
   Aberdeen Bazar
   Port Blair 744101
   Te.Ph. 33358, 33034

2. Shiva Laxmi Tours and Travel Agency
   Aberdeen Bazar
   Port Blair 744101
   Te.Ph. 33723

3. Laxmi Motors,
   Aberdeen Bazar
   Port Blair
   Tel.Ph. 33826, 33070

4. Miduna Travels
   5, Middle Point
   Port Blair 744101
   Tel.Ph. 33028, 32360, 32425.

5. Shompen Travels.
   2 Middle Point
   Port Blair 744101
   Tel.Ph. 33028, 32360, 32425.

6. Wheels -Rent a Car
   Middle Point
   Port Blair 744101
   Tel.Ph. 32704.

Tourist Guides : Tourist's, both domestic and foreign, come from different parts of India and other countries. They speak different languages and belong to different cultures. They visit A&N Islands with an intention to know a lot about this destination. Tourists will be able to make their visit of Andaman markable and purposeful only when they understand clearly about the history of this place, social importance of these places, the places of interest, particulars about the tribals, national memoirs etc. Of course, at some important places, a brief of about places, persons is given in Hindi and English but all tourists can not be expected to know all the languages. A tourist will not be able to understand every aspect about A&N Islands in a short period without a knowledgeable person to guide him. So tourists need the help of some persons or a person who has full knowledge about the destination. Such a person is called a Tourist Guide. He should know many languages, be accommodative, have some valuable personal qualities like freshness, wit, smiling face, good knowledge of the places, national memoirs, beachces, hotels etc. The behaviour of the guide towards the tourists should be friendly. He should lead them as a friend without showing any partiality towards any one. So a tourist guide can really contribute to the growth of tourism Industry in A&N Islands. In Port Blair a list of approved guides is maintained by the Govt.of India tourism office. The number of such trained guides is 9. Approved tourists guides may be hired through Govt.of India tourists Office, Junglighat, Port Blair. Lists of tourist guides and rates are given in Table 5. 21 and 5.22.

Table 5.21
List of Approved Tourist Guides

Sl.No.	Name	Telephone Number
1.	Shri Neeraj Kumar Balaiya	32984
2.	Kum. E.Everlyn	32984
3.	Shri Sammed Ali	33556
4.	Shri Raj Kumar Chaurasia	30058
5.	Shri C.H.Hemant Rao	32984/32800
6.	Kum Rishi Kala	85253
7.	Shri Anil Koshy	32839
8.	Shri Sankar	33931
9.	Shri M.G. Srinivasalu	33897

Source :- Tourist Office, Govt. of India, Janglighat, Port Blair.

Table 5.22
Revised Rates of Tourist Guides w.e.f. 1.10.96

Sl.No. Day	1-4 Persons	5-15 persons	15-35 persons
	(Inclusive of Transport & Allowances)		
1. Half Day (1-4 hrs)	Rs.230/-	Rs.345/-	Rs.460/-
2. Full Day (Upto 8 hrs)	Rs.345/-	Rs.460/-	Rs.750/-

i) Over 35 persons - two guides or Rs.20/- per person extra.
ii) Language allowance per day - Rs.100/-
iii) Outstation Allowances Rs. 850/- per night
iv) When a travel agent/tour operator/excursion agent provides hotel accommodation and meals in the same hotel where the clients are staying and bearing expenses, the outstation allowances will be only to Rs.300/- per night.

Source :- Govt.of India Tourist Office,Port Blair.

OTHER FACILITIES

Shopping : Shopping is another important activity of the tourists. They feel relaxed when they go for shopping. They want to buy and take the product which is the speciality of the particular destination. Port Blair city is very famous for a variety of handicrafts. Both Indian tourists and foreign tourists purchase the handicrafts and present the same to their kith and kin, friends and relatives, teachers and students, doctors and patients, temples, mosques, churches, gurudhuwaras as the symbol of their visit to this lush green paradise with a pride that it is made in A&N Islands. Some tourists keep the product as the show piece in their own house as a matter of prestige. Dancing dolls of different varieties, shell lamps, shell decoratives, shell hanging lamps, saree tops, table weights, shell saucers,pen stands, timber-made fish turtles, eagles, dinosaurs, shell-made rings, nacklace, kumkum, pots etc. are very famous and specialised items of these islands. Tourists spend a lot of amount on shopping but comparatively less than the other part of their expenses. After the shopping is over, tourists can enjoy Andaman special "samosa" infront of Mount Batten theatre, Middle Point, Port Blair and Andaman Special pan almost in every shop.

Water Sports : In A&N Islands there is no river which can provide boating facility to the tourists. But for the purpose of boating there are water sports complexes available in the Port Blair city. Shippighat water sports complex,Gandhi Park Water Sports complex Andaman water sports complex, Carbynscove tourism complex are the famous water sports' complexes. Of these, Shippighat water sports complex is managed by sports Authority of India (SAI) in order to train the local youth in water sports like, Kayaking,Canoeing, Sailing, Swimming and other sports activities. At present, the Shippighat complex offers water sports faciltiy to the tourists also. Children below 5 years are not allowed or permitted. The Gandhi Park Water Sports Complex and Andaman Water Sports Complex are oraganised and managed by the department of tourism, A&N Administration. All these water sports facilties are provided on all days. There are two types of water sports namely, safe water sports and adventure water sports. The timings for the water sports are as follows :

1. Safe water sports	8.00 hrs—20.00hrs (8.00 AM to 8.00 PM)
2. Adventure water sports	8.00 hrs — 17.00 hrs (8.00 AM to 5 .00 PM)

Two seater paddle boats, four seater paddle boats, kayaks, rowing boats, motor boats, sail yachts etc. are the types of boats given to the tourists at very nominal rates for half-an-hour duration. Snorkels, life jackets, life buoys are also available in the complexes. The telephone numbers to be contacted are 30799 & 30898.

Clubs/Associations : Clubs are also contributing their valuable services to the promotion of Tourism Industry. In A&N Islands the important clubs are Tamizar Snagam, Bengali Club, Lions Club, Rotary Club, Rotrac Club, NGO's Association, ACTA, Kerala Samgam, YMCA, Maharastra Mandal, Andhra Association, Hindi Sahitya Kala Parishada and Kannada Sangam etc. All clubs have membership fees.These associations / clubs organise may functions, speeches, talks and programmes highlighting the socio cultural economic activities of these Islands. They invite scholars from the mainland and entertain them.They organise sports competition activity, participate in special regional festivals like Chitra Vizha, Thiruvalluvar Vizha, Durga Puja, Pongal Vizha, literary talks etc., with some cultural programmes. Tourists from the particular regions go and witness or even sometimes participate in the programme.

Swimming Pool : Till 1994, A&N Islands, the city has only one salt water swimming pool which was constructed inside the sea. One can swim in the pool when there is favourable tide. The Lt.Governor of A&N Island has initiated and constructed another swimming pool inside the Jimkhanna ground. It is very beautiful looking,has international standard and is really a wonderful facility provided to the tourists. It is situated in just 1km from bus terminus. Beside these swimming pools, the hotel Bay Island of welcome group also has swimming pool faciltiy.

Banks : There are 11 banks-10 commercial banks and one Cooperative Bank - with all the facilities in A&N Islands They have their own branches in different Islands.These banks are SBI, Canara Bank, Syndicate Bank, Indian Overseas Bank, United Bank, UCO Bank, Punjab National Bank, Vijaya Bank, Andaman State Cooperative Bank, Indian Bank, Allahabad Bank. The facility of exchanging foreign currency is limited to the main branch of State Bank of India and Indian Overseas Bank. The other hotel organisations namely Hotel Bay Island, Sinclairs bay view Hotel Pearless Resort, Hotel Shompen also have the facility of exchanging foreign currencies and accepting the travellers' cheque.

Post and Telegraph : Post and telegraph is the nervous system of any country and it is considered the most important for the A&N Islands. Here people live only on the effective working of the post and telegraph system.The city Port Blair has only one head Post office. But the working hours of this post office are from 9.00 AM to 5.00 PM. There are 33 sub post offices and 64 branches of Post Office with 244 letter boxes. Only one telegraphic office is situated in the Port Blair city. The other Post Offices have the facility of booking telegrams. Inter-Islands urgent messages are passed through wirelss and signal system.

Hospitals : Hospitals/Medical facilities are provided by the A&N Administration through the Department of Health, headed by the Director of Health Services. G.B.Pant Hospital is the biggest hospital with all its facilities situated in Port Blair just behind the Cellular Jail. Besides this hospital, there are amenities like Primary Health Centre, Community Health Centres, Sub-Centres, Dispensary, Urban Health Centre, functioning in the different places of these islands. The doctors working in these hospitals and centres are prohibited to practice privately. Medical facilities, provided by the health department, are free including medicines and injections. X-ray, Ecg etc. Serious patients of inter-islands who require special and specialised treatment are sent to the nearest specialised hospital or to Port Blair G.B.Pant Hospital either by special boat or by helicoper. In case of problematic conditions, they are sent to mainland hospitals (Chennai or Calcutta). Till recent past there were no private hospitals in these islands. But of late, the private clinics have come up with relatively less facilities for the emergency treatment.

Cinema : Cinema is an important means of enterainment, particularly for home tourists. But in A&N Islands there are no cinema studios and professional shooting is not done here. The films are brought from the mainland and screened in these islands (only in the city). From the tourists' point of view there are only 5 cinema threatres in this territory and all are situated in Port Blair city only. No cinema hall is meant for any particular regional movies. All halls show all movies in all languages. All cinema halls hold three shows daily. Tamil, Hindi, movies are shown more. Other language movies are occassional. English movies are comparitively rare. The names and addresses of the Cinema halls are:-

1.	Mount Batten Talkies Port Blair 744101 Tel.Ph. 32293	-	Middle Point.
2.	Light House Near LIC Building Mahatma Gandhi Road Port Blair -744101 Tel.Ph. 33344.	-	Gandhi Nagar
3.	Anand Paradis Port Blair 744104 Tel.Ph. 32311	-	School Line
4.	Ansari Talkies Port Blair 744103	-	Dairy Farm
5.	Dweepika Hall (Restricted Indian Navy)	-	Buniyadabad Haddo-744102.
6.	Swapna Theatre		Dollygunj

Photography : Photography occupies an important place in tourism activity. Tourists do not get full satisfaction if they have not taken photos of the important places liked by them. Some tourists would like to have immediate developing and printing. Here in Andamans, Photo studios,

Photographers, Private video operators, Video filming facilities are available. A beautiful colour lab and processing unit named Nice Colour Lab attached with New Prabhat Studio is in Delanipur junction, just 1/2 km from Port Blair bus terminus. Films are processed, developed and printed within 1 hr. Films, suitable for all cameras, are available in Andamans. There is no restriction on taking photographs except in tribal areas and some vital installations. The addresses of the photographers and studios are

1. Studio Monalisa
   Dairy Farm
   Port Blair- 744103
2. New Prabhat Studio
   Junglighat
   Port Blair 744103
3. Das Studio
   Junglighat
   Port Blair 744103
   PH: 33415
4. Sapna Studio
   Aberdeen Bazar
   Port Blair 744101
   PH: 32861
5. Sapna Colour Lab and Video Division
   Gurunanak Market
   Aberdeen Bazar
6. Nithya Colour Lab
   Middle Point
   Port Blair 744101
7. Somu Studio
   Aberdeen Bazar

Port Blair 744101
PH: 33045, 33938.

8. Central Studio Colour Lab and Video Div.
Light House Building
Maulana Azad Road, Port Blair 744101, PH: 33326.
9. New Prabhat Studio
Delanipur
Port Blair 744102.
PH: 32944

6

GROWTH OF TOURISM

In the previous chapter, tourism facilities available in A&N Islands were discussed in detail by dividing the total facilities as basic facilities, supporting facilities and other facilities. It is understood by all the sectors of the A &N Islands that the infant industry tourism is to be developed by giving all booster doses. Moreover, the Govt. of India has declared these islands as industrially backward areas. The then Lt.Governor (Administrator) of A&N Islands, on the recommendations of the Ministry of Tourism, Govt. of India, New Delhi passed an order that "Tourism" is to be treated as Industry in A&N islands by announcing concessions, subsidies etc. The author has also delivered a talk in the All India Radio on the topic "Beyond Kalapani" broadcasted on 24th October, 1996 at 20.20 Hrs. in which he has clearly mentioned that the Tourism is the only possible sector that can be developed in these islands. He expressed that the tourism is an accelerator, as far as these islands are concerned, to the economic growth. The number of tourists both Indian and Foreign to these islands has also been increasing. So in this chapter, an attempt has been made to study the growth of tourism in A & N islands, by taking the number of tourists' arrival every year during the plan periods and by taking the total amount of investment made by the A&N Administration on the infrastructural facilities necessary for tourism industry.

TOURISM SEASON

The weather conditions of A&N islands have its own peculier nature. These islands do not always have parallel climatic conditions. Some-time there is heavy rain in Andaman district but at that time there is no rain in Nicobar district. These islands always have tropical weather but, generally pleasant throughout the year with a minimum temperature of 23°C and maximum of 30°C Humidity is always high, i.e. from 70% to 90% with gentle breeze blowing all the time. The average rain fall is at 3000mm. Geographically, the weather conditions may be classified as winter, summer, rainy etc. But in the present work, the whole weather is divided into two namely Tourists Season and Non Tourist Season (Off-Season). But strictly speaking, even in Non Tourist season i.e. in Off-Season, comparatively less number of visitors come to these islands. Normally, every year these islands have heavy rainfall during the period from May to mid of September and slight rainfall from mid of November to first week of December. This is due to two monsoons namely South West and North East. So the best season for tourists to visit these islands (almost all the islands) is from October to May. The remaining period from May to September is also not a bad time to visit these islands. But generally, tourists don't come so often to these islands during this period. So the period between October and May is called Tourist Season and the period between May and September is called Off-Season. The weather conditions of every day are given in the Table 6.1 from the tourist's point of view by mentioning P- for Pleasant S - for Sunlight, R - for Rain, Ex - Excellent.

FACTORS FAVOURING GROWTH

Tourism industry in these Bay Islands is a healthy infant industry from the point of view of tourists, their time available, amount of income and free mobility decide the destination. The people will travel on large scale if their time, income, mobility are at their discretion. A survey

Table 6.1
Daily Weather Conditions from the Tourist's Point of view

Month	Every day During					
	3-4 am	4-10 am	10am-3pm	3-5 pm	5-8 pm	8pm-3am
January	P	S	S	P	P	P
February	P	P&S	P&S	P&S	P	P
March	P	P&S	P&S	P&S	P	P
April	P	P&S	P&S	P&S	P	P
May	R	R	R	R	R	R
June	R	R	R	R	R	R
July	R	R	R	R	R	R
August	P	R	R	P	P	R
September	P	P	R	R	P	R
October	Ex	Ex	S	S	Ex	Ex
November	Ex	Ex	R	R	Ex	Ex
December	R	Ex	S	P&S	Ex	Ex

Source: Personal experience

proves that the people having discretionary income give preference to tourism and travel rather than purchasing consumer durables or making long term investment. The main factors favouring the growth of tourism in A & N islands, besides the above , are:

1. Never ending Natural Scenic beauty of this Green Paradise
2. Pollutionless, free natural way of valuable life, free from gundaism, riots, burglary and political evils and politics-free life.
3. A most hospitable and cosmopolitan society, free from the rigidities of caste, creed and religion, projecting Indian culture and unity in diversity in A & N islands.
4. Increased transport facilities, not only between Mainland - Island but also between islands.
5. Increased accommodation facilities for different classes of people.
6. Selective publicity through the educational publishers like Manas Publishers who are showing keen interest in the development of these Mari-Gold Islands.

CLASSIFICATION

The trend in the growth of tourism in the.A&N islands is discussed under the following headings namely,

1. Domestic Tourism
2. Foreign Tourism
3. Total Tourism
4. Tourism during Plan Periods
5. Investment on Tourism.

All the relevant required data to trace the growth of tourism was not available. Only the number of tourists arrived on these islands, and the amount of investment made on the tourism industry by the A & N islands were available. These data were analysed in the maximum possible ways and presented.

Domestic Tourism

Though the Tourism Industry as a whole i.e both Domestic Tourism and Foreign Tourism and its development are very essential to this territory, domestic tourism forms an integral part of this Island Tourism. As it is already mentioned that A & N Islands is a mini India due to the amazing racial and cultural mix, people from all regions, religions are living in this territory. Here in this mini Indian paradise, the inter-religion, and inter-region marriages are common. Hence, the place like A & N islands with different socio economic and cultural patterns, the promotion of domestic tourism would defintely increase and encourage the unity in diversity, a fundamental base and necessity for National Integration. Domestic tourism increases the possibility of peace through understanding among the divergent sectors in the population. In fact, development of foreign tourism is possible only if the domestic tourism has a strong and fast growth. Hence an attempt has been made to trace the growth of domestic tourism in A & N islands by taking down the number of tourists arrived. Table 6.2 shows the year-wise number of tourists who arrived into these islands.

Table 6.2
Domestic Tourists arrivals in A&N islands (In No)

Year	No. of Tourists	Growth rate over the Previous Year (in%)
1978	3750	-
1979	4050	8.0
1980	7500	85.2
1981	8835	17.8
1982	13444	52.2
1983	14020	4.3
1984	16000	14.1
1985	20942	30.9
1986	20942	-
1987	31591	50.8
1988	34589	9.5
1989	39967	15.6
1990	27019	(-)32.4
1991	32242	19.3
1992	35817	11.1
1993	35000	(-)2.3
1994	50737	45.0
1995	64490	27.1

Source: Tourism Department, A&N Administration Port Blair

The table reveals that the arrival of DTs hast been increasing regularly. High rate of growth was recorded in the years 1980,1982,1985, 1987 1994 and 1995. The main reason for this high rate of increase from the year 1980 onwards is the introduction of air service. The Indian Airlines started direct air service operation of Boeing 737 aircrafts from Calcutta to Port Blair with effect from 2nd August 1977. The frequency has been increased from 1979-80 onwards. Before the introduction of the direct air service i.e. Boeing 737 aircrafts, Viscount aircrafts were operated. These aircrafts had to touch Rangoon, the Capital of Burma, for some technical reasons. Due to this stop-over, the journey time between Calcutta and Port Blair was about 5 hours. Also, the Indian Airlines started the air services between Port Blair and Madras with effect from November 1982 without any stop-over problem. Now the journey time between PortBlair and Madras is only 2 hrs & 10 min. and also between the Port Blair and Calcutta is 2 hrs. The other reasons are that the frequency of the voyages by ships between Mainland and Port Blair has increased during these years. The table also recorded a negative growth rate of 32.4% in the year 1990, and a slight negative growth rate of 2.3% in the year 1993. The reasons attributed to this is that during these years there was a frequeant cancellation of ships and flights, strikes etc. However, one can see the regular growth in the number of tourists' arrivals on these islands. The table also pictures that there is a good scope for the development of tourism industry in these islands.

Foreign Tourism

Today the economic, political, social and cultural environment of the world has become so complicated. Though understanding among the people, the exchange of their views and thoughts on economic, political and socio-cultural issues are absolutely essential in the present day situation peace among the people of a village, town, city, district, state and country and countries and the world as a "whole" should be manufactured, produced and fabricated. This is possible only by the smokeless industry "Tourism". Even for tangible products, the nations, no doubt, depend on each other by extending their help to others within the meaning of the Principle of Comparitive Advantage. Foreign Tourism plays an important role both directly and indirectly in promoting the international trade in earning foreign exchange, settling of balance of payments position and in international understanding. Besides, foreign exchange, as it is already mentioned, the foreign tourism by its tourism multiplier effect will stimulate the employment generation, income generation, development of local growth

Centres etc. The Table No.6.3 shows the year-wise number of FTs who arrived into A&N Islands.

Table 6.3
Foreign Tourists' arrivals in A & N islands

Year	No. of Tourists	Growth rate over the Previous year (in %)
1978	250	-
1979	347	38.8
1980	2096	504.0
1981	1170	(-) 44.2
1982	1102	(-) 5.8
1983	1817	64.9
1984	3152	73.5
1985	1264	(-) 59.9
1986	1792	41.7
1987	2085	16.4
1988	3663	75.7
1989	2392	34.7
1990	6697	180.0
1991	2248	(-) 66.4
1992	2435	8.3
1993	1771	(-) 27.3
1994	3798	114.5
1995	3849	1.3

Source: Tourism Department, Port Blair & Basic Statistics, A & N Admn.

From the table it is clear that the growth in the arrival of FTs is not regular. This is becasue of the policy matters of the respective countries. However, the high rates of changes were recorded in the arrival of foreign tourists in the years 1980, 1984, 1988, 1989, 1990, 1991, 1992 1994 and 1995. But the growth is zig zag from the year 1978 to 1986 but from the year 1987 onwards the growth is somewhat regular. When comparing the years prior to 1987, the years post 1987 recorded a significant growth particularly in the years 1987, 1988, 1990,1992,1994 and 1995.

The number of Foreign Tourists, arrived in the year 1978 was 250 which rose to 3152 in 1984, to 6697 in 1990 and 3849 in 1995, recording an increase of 13 times(1160.8%), 27 times and 16 times for a period of 6 years, 12 years and 18 years respectively. During 1979, the growth rate was 38.8% over the previous year whereas in the next year it went upto a markable growth rate of 504%. Other significant growth rates were recorded in the year 1983 as 64.9%, in 1984 as 73.5%, in 1988 as 75.7% and in 1990 as 180.0% The table recorded a negative growth rates in the years 1981, 1982,1985, 1989, 1991 and 1993. Frequent hikes in the passenger fare in the transport both for ships and flights, non- availability of ships and flights, frequent changes in the shipping programmes, sudden diversion of the ships to some other destinations etc. are the reasons attributed for such negative growth rates. One more reason for the negative growth rate is the sudden stoppage of Russian Tourists into A & N islands due to their internal problems However, though the number of foreign tourists, arrived into A & N islands, seems to have decreased, it is evident from the table when comparing it with the initial years, that there has been slight increase in the number of foreign tourists.

Total Number of Tourists' Arrival

Growth of Domestic Tourists and Foreign Tourists has been separately traced out with the graphs and diagrams etc. With a view' to have a bird's eye view on the total number of tourists, arrived into these islands, the total number of tourists arrived is given in the Table 6.4

It is clear from the above table that the number of tourists, arrived into these islands, has been increasing since 1978 onwards except in 1990. The reasons for the increase and decrease in the number of tourists have already been analysed in the light of the growth of Domestic Tourism and Foreign Tourism. Growth in total number of tourists arrived into these islands has been on the Increase.

Table 6.4
Total Number of Tourists Arrived Into A&N Islands

Total Number of Tourists		% Increase over the Previous Year
1978	4000	-
1979	4397	9.9
1980	9596	118.2
1981	10005	4.3
1982	14546	45.4
1983	15837	8.9
1984	19152	20.9
1985	22555	17.8
1986	22733	0.8
1987	33676	48.1
1988	38252	13.6
1989	42359	10.7
1990	33716	20.4 (-)
1991	34490	2.3
1992	38252	10.9
1993	36771	3.9(-)
1994	54535	48.3
1995	68339	25.3

Source: Tourism Department , A&N Administration, Port Blair.

Negative growth has been recorded in the year 1990 and 1993. The main reasons are frequent changes and cancellations of ship and flights. Another reason is the decrease in the number of tourists from USSR. The variation in the number of foreign tourists is also one of the reasons for the fluctuations in the growth of total tourists. Declaration of Tourism as Industry in these islands by giving all benefits such as concessions, subsidies, incentives etc, by the then Lt. Governor of A&N islands during the year 1987 was the main favourable reason for the growth of tourism, particularly domestic tourism. A lot of hotels, restaurants, tourism facilities, lodges, tour operators, travel agents, transport came into existence only after the declaration of tourism as industry.

Growth During the Plan Periods

Data on the number of tourists arrived into these islands are available from 1978 onwards whereas for the plan periods, it is available/only from the Annual Plan 1979-80 onwards. Another scale has been taken to trace out the growth of tourism in these islands. That is the total amount of expenditure invested on the development of Tourism in those islands. The data on the amount of expenditure could be collected only from the III Five Year Plan onwards. So the growth during the plan periods has been traced and presented under two headings namely. "number of tourists arrived" and "the amount of investment on the tourism in these islands".

Number of Tourists' Arrivals : Table No.6.5 shows the arrival of Foreign Tourists and Domestic Tourists, into these island in terms of number during the plan periods, from the Annual Plan 1979-80 onwards.

TABLE 6.5
Number of Tourists' Arrival in A& N Islands During Plan Period

Sl. No	Plan Periods	Foreign Tourists	Doemetic Tourists	Total Tourists	Average Annual Arrival
1.	Annual Plan1979-80	8800	597	9397	9397
2.	VI Five Year Plan	59799	9337	69136	13827
3.	VII Five Year Plan	148031	11722	159753	31951
4.	Annual Plan 1990-91	27997	5754	33751	33751
5.	Annual P1991-92	36637	1829	38466	38466
6.	VIII five Year Plan*	196884	13167	210051	52513

Source: Tourism Department, A & N Administration, Port Blair.

The table clearly reveals that during the Plan periods tourists' visits to these islands have been increasing. The number of tourists, arrived in total i.e. Average Annual

Arrival (AAA) 9397, consisting of 8800 DTs and 597 FTs in annual plan period 1979-80 increased to 13827, the Average Annual Arrival for the VI Plan period, recording a significant growth of 47.1%. This includes the AAA of 11960 of DTs and 1867 FTs with a growth rate of 35.9% and 212.7% respectively. Remarkable growth of tourists' arrival has been recorded during the VII Five Year Plan i.e 1985-90 when compared to VI Five Year Plan. The AAA of 13827 consists of 11960 DTs and 1867 FTs during the VI Five Year Plan period having grown upto AM of 31951 consists of 29606 DTs and 2345 FTs during the VII Five Year Plan Period of 1985-90 marked a growth rate of 147.5% in DTs, 25.6% in FTs and 131.1% on overall total tourists. The VII Five Year Plan Period was really the period in which the tourist industry was accelerated. Moreover, the expenditure during VI Five Year Plan has brought a good result in the VII Five Year Plan Period. The annual expenditure during the VI Plan Period was 14.45 lakhs, increased from 9.2 lakhs in the previous year to the Plan Period. The same amount of expenditure continued in the next five year plan also i.e. VII Plan. Both capital and the expenditure has recorded a significant growth during the Annual Plan Period 90-91 1991-92. Though the number of DTs came down to 27997 during the year 1990-91 from AAA of 29609 of VII Plan Period by recording negative growth of 5.4%, increased to 36637 during 1991-92 by making phenomenal growth of 30.9%. But in case of FTs, it was increased to 5754 during the Annual Plan 1990-91 from AAA of 2349 during the VII Plan by recording a significant growth of 145%. But at the same time during the Annual Plan 1991-92, the number of FTs , arrived into these islands, came down to 1829 with a negative growth rate of 68.2%. The reason, attributed for this is the sudden hike of airfare, non availability of ships and frequeant cancellation of shipping programmes etc. At present, more number of tourists visit these islands particularly DTs and FTs too. AAA for VIII Five Year Plan has been increased to 52513, consisting of 49221 DTs and 3292 FTs by recording a growth of 36.5% in total, 34.5% in DTs and 80% FTs over the Annual Plan Period of 1991-92. When compared with the Annual Plan of 1979-80, the growth at present is something marvellous. Arrival of DTs during the Annual Plan 1979-80 was 8800 which rose to 49221(AAA) during the VIII Five Year Plan Period This is near about 6 times i.e. 559.3%, and that of FTs, 597 rose to 3292 which is also about 6 times i.e. 551.4% and so is the case of total tourists, arrived during the same periods. The reasons for such marked growth is the expenditure increased or the amount invested in order to develop the tourism industry by the A & N islands.

Tourism Expenditure

The analysation on the growth of tourism during plan periods with the help of the number of tourists, arrived into these islands, clearly reveals that the expenditure incurred by the A & N Administration on the development of the tourism industry in these islands is also one of the reasons for the growth of the industry. So, an analysis has also been made to trace the growth by taking the total expenditure as the basis. Table 6.6. shows the amount of expenditure incurred by the A & N Administration during the Plan Periods.

The above table clearly conveys that the expenditure during the Plan periods and Annual Average Expenditure (AAE) for the periods has been increasing. The total expenditure on tourism in the VIII th Five year Plan Period upto 1996 is 1643.37 lakhs with the AAE of Rs. 410.84 lakhs which was only 76.88 lakh during the Annual Plan period 1991-92, and Rs. 32.2 during the Annual Plan 1990-91. The growth of expenditure (AAE) i about 13 times compared to periods' Annual Plan 1990-91 and VIIIth Five Plan Period and the same is about 6 times when compared with the Annual Plan 1991-92. This expenditure includes the construction of tourists accommodation, Yatri Niwas, Tourist Home, Development of Water Sports, Recreational Tourism, Beautification of

Table 6.6
Tourism Expenditure by A&N Administration During Plan Periods

Sl.No.	Plan Periods	Actual Expenditure (in Rs.'000)	Average Annual Expenditure per year in Rs. '000
1.	III Five Year Plan - 1961-66	325.0	65.0
2.	IV Five Year Plan - 1969-74	297.0	59.4
3.	V Five Year Plan - 1974-79	1870.0	374.0
4.	Annual Plan - 1979-80	924.0	924.0
5.	Five Year Plan - 1080-85	7251.0	1450.2
6.	VII Five Year Plan - 1985-90	7254.0	1450.8
7.	Annual Plan - 1990-91	3220.0	3220.0
8.	Annual Plan - 1991-92	7688.0	7688.0
9.	VIII Five Year Plan- 1992-97*	164337.0	41084.0

Source: Tourism Department, A & N Administration, Port Blair. 1996
*upto 1996 only

Tourist Spots, etc. All expenses are of capital nature which makes one believe that it will bring about good results in future. By taking the number of tourists, arriving in these islands, into account from the Plan Period year 1978 onwards, it is evident from the Table 6.5 that it is increasing every year. 'The Average Annual Expenditure during the IV Plan Period Rs. 59.4 thousands increased to 374 thousands in the V Plan Period and to 924 thousands in the Annual Plan year. The Annual Average Expenditure of Rs. 1450.2 thousands in the VI Plan period has increased with a slight change of 0.6 thousands in the next five year plan but increased to Rs. 3220 thousands in the Annual Plan Period 1990-91, 7688 thousands in Annual Plan Period 1991-92 and Rs. 41084 thousands in the current five year plan 1992-97 with a corresponding increase in the number of tourists during this period which can be seen from the Table 6.5. This micro level analysation reveals a fact that if the A & N Islands is developed, it can attract more number of tourists.

7

TOURISTS VIEWS AND SATISFACTION

Growth of Tourism depends directly on the tourism development of the destination. Again the tourism development depends on the tourism policy, if any, adopted by the State/Govt. To strengthen and update the policy if anything already in existence, and if not, to make a fresh tourism policy, understanding the characteristics of the tourists, their ideas, source of information to them, length of stay, their views and level of satisfaction and their problems are very important. So an attempt has been made in this chapter to elicit the views and satisfaction of the tourists who have visited these islands.

METHODOLOGY

The data has been collected by personal contacts and sample surveys. By selecting a sample group, a semi structured questionnaire was served after having a proper pilot study. All questionnaires were filled up by the tourists only when they were about to leave these islands after completion of their visit. That was just one or two days before starting their journey to the mainland. Totally 150 Domestic Tourists (DTs), 75 Foreign Tourists (FTs) were selected as a sample group and the questionnaires issued to them. Among them, 142 DTs and 57 FTs could find time to concentrate on the questionnaire. Out of 142 DTs and 57 FTs, 12 DTs and 7

FTs filledup partly. So after leaving these partly answered questionnaires, the remaining 130 DTs and 50 FTs have been taken for this analysis. This is shown in Table 7.1.

Table 7.1
Particulars of Sample Group

	Particulars	Number of DT s	FT s	Total
1.	Questionnaires Supplied	150	75	225
2.	Questionnaires Collected	142	57	199
3.	Partly filled up	12	7	19
4.	Fully filled up	130	50	180
5.	Questionnaires taken for the study	130	50	180

Information from the questionnaires have been tabulated, interpreted with discussion and presented here.

CLASSIFICATION

The total information, collected as above, have been analysed by classifying the same into three major headings namely,

(a) Personal Data
(b) On-the-Travel Data and
(c) Data on Views and Satisfaction

They are further classified as follows:

(a) Personal Data
- i) Age Group
- ii) Sex Group
- iii) Occupational Group
- iv) Income Group

(b) On-the-Travel Data
- i) Source of Informat ion
- ii) Mode of Travel
- iii) Purpose of Visit
- iv) Length of Stay

v) Helping Means of Travel
vi) Modes of Transport for inter-islands
vii) Places of Stay

(c) Data on Views and Satisfaction
i) About Journey from Mainland
ii) Level of Satisfaction about Transport
iii) Views about Accommodation
iv) Level of Satisfaction
v) About Food
vi) Level of Satisfaction
vii) About Bar
viii) About Price level
ix) About Tourist Attractions
x) About Tourism Supporting facilities

The above classification is discussed in detail.

PERSONAL DATA

Age Group : For a planner of Tourism Industry, a thorough understanding about the tourists is a primary necessity. Which age group? which sex group? etc. interested in tourism are to be understood properly. Likes and dislikes, according to their age, sex, education etc, are to be found out. Without analysing all these factors, if plans are made, the tourism industry will fall sick and the amount invested for will also be depreciated. So an attempt has been made to study these aspects of the tourists. Table No.7.2 shows the age group of the respondents(tourists).

The following table reveals that out of total respondents consisting of 50 Foreign Tourists(FT) and 130 Domestic Tourists(DT), maximum number of tourists belong to the age group of 20-50 years. Out of 180 respondents, 150 respondents representing 83.3% fall under the age group of 20-50 years. Among this age group, tourists between 20-40 years show much more interest in travel. Out of 150 respondents, 86 representing 47.7%(to the total) fall under the age group of 20-40 years. But among the FT, as per the table, the age group 40-50 years show more interest in tourism. That is 22 respondents representing 44.0% to the total FT belong to the age group 40-50 years. The table also reveals that the age group below 20 years and above 50 years do not show much interest in tourism.

Table 7.2
Age Group of the Tourists

	Number of respondents(tourists)		
Age Group	Domestic Tourists	Foreign Tourists	Total
Below 20 years	8(72.2) (6.2)	3(27.3) (6.0)	11(100.0) (6.1)
20 - 40 years	68(79.1) (52.3)	18(20.9) (36.0)	86((100.0) (47.7)
40 - 50 years	42(65.6) (32.3)	22(34.4) (44.0)	64(100.0) (35.6)
50 years and above	12(63.2) (9.2)	7(36.8) (14.0)	19(100.0) (10.6)
Total	130(72.2) (100.0)	50(27.8) (100.0)	180(100.0) (100.0)

Source: Primary Data

Sex Group : Next to age, sex of the tourists occupies an important position in this smokeless industry. Table 7.3 shows the sex-wise tourists respondents.

Table 7.3
Sex Group of Tourists

Sex	Number of Tourists/Respondents		
	DT	FT	Total
Male	90(77.6) (69.2)	26(22.4) (52.0)	116(100.0) (64.4)
Female	40(62.5) (30.8)	24(37.5) (48.0)	64(100.0) (35.6)
Total	130(72.2) (100.0)	50(27.8) (100.0)	180(100.0) (100.0)

Source: Primary Data

As per the Table 7.3, out of 180 respondents 116

representing 64.4% are males and the remaining 64 representing 35.6% are females. As far as the domestic tourists are concerned, 90 out of 130 i.e. 69.2% are males and 'the remaining 40 out of 130 i.e. 30.8% are females. Whereas among the foreign tourists, 26 out of 50 i.e. 52% are males and the remaining 24 i.e. 48% are females. It is clear from the table, that the FTs go for tourism by giving equal importance to females because the ratio between male females is 52%. 48% i.e. almost equal whereas the Indian tourists go for tourism by giving less importance to the females because the ratio between male female is 69% : 30%.

Occupational Group : Occupation of the tourists plays a vital role in the growth of tourism. The status of the tourism fully depends on the occupational pattern of the tourists. Cheap tourism will be a dangerous phenomena for the overall tourism industry in these islands. Hence understaing the occuapational patterns of the tourists visiting this A&N &slands has become a prerequiste. Table 7.4 shows the occupational pattern of the tourists who visited these islands.

Table 7.4
Occupations of the Respondents /Tourists

Occupations	Number of Respondens/Tourists		
	DT	FT	Total
Students	12(63.2) (9.2)	7(36.8) (14.0)	19(100.0) (10.6)
Employees	37(61.7) (28.5)	23(38.3) (46.0)	60(100.0) (33.3)
Business/Professionals	78(81.3) (60.0)	18(18.7) (36.0)	96(100.0) (53.3)
Others	03(60.0) (2.8)	02(40.0) (4.0)	05(100.0) (2.8)
Total	130(72.2) (100.0)	50(27.8) (100.0)	80(100.0) (100.0)

Source : Primary data.

The above table reveals that the maximum numbei of tourists to these islands come from the Business and professional occupations of the total sample, 96 tourists representing 53.3% are from the business and professionals' group. This is followed by the employee's group i.e 60 tourists representing 33.3% as employees. Professionals include doctors, lawyers, auditors, engineers, architects, artists etc. Others include retired persons, widows, agriculturists, unemployed etc. When compared the DTs who contribute a large number from business and profession, i.e. are about 60% of the total DTs, the FTs from the employees group i.e. 46% followed by business group. The students' group has been recorded only 10.5% consisting of 9.2% DT and 14% FT of their respective totals. The great significance of this table is that it gives positive symptoms of the strong prospects of rich tourism in A & N islands as about 90% of the respondents are from the employees, business and professionals' group.

Income of the Tourists : As far as the income of the respondents is concerned, nobody submitted the correct data. That's why that particular aspect is not discussed and hence it is deleted. However it is understood from the discussion that all the tourists, atleast, those who are falling under employees, business & professionals' groups have very good income.

ON-THE-TRAVEL DATA

Source of Information : After the personal data on age, sex occupation and the income of the respondent tourists have been analysed, some information about the tourism, mode of travel, source of information, etc. were asked and analysed. For a succesful tourism activity, the tourists are to be given a correct information and it should be authentic, reliable and purposeful. Table 7.5 shows the source of information to the tourists.

The following table reveals that their own intuition/interest and the friends and relatives are the important source of information to the tourists who have visited these islands. Nintey nine representing 55% of the total respondents consisting of 58 (44.6%) DTs and 41(82%) FTs have expressed that they come to these islands on their own interest and intuition. Seventy five representing 42% of the total tourists consisting of 72(55.4%) DTs and 3(6%) FTs have told that they got information about A & N islands through their friends and relatives. The table clearly pictures that DTs could not get any information through the Tourists office in the Mainland whereas 6 FTs representing 12% of the total FTs and 0.03% of the Total Tourists show that their source of information is the Tourist Office. It is also clear from the table that no advertisement is being given in order to promote tourism in these islands.

Table 7.5
Source of information to the Respondent Tourists

Source of Information	No.of Respondents/Tourists		
	DT	FT	Total
Friends & Relatives	72(96.0) (55.4)	03(4.0) (6.0)	75(100.0) (41.7)
Own Intuition/Interest	58(58.6) (44.6)	41(41.4) (82.0)	99(100.0) (55.0)
Tourist Office	–	06(100.0) (12.0)	06(100.0) (3.3)
Advertisements/Literature	-	-	-
Others	-	-	-
Total	130(72.2) (100.0)	50(27.8) (100.0)	180(100.0) (100.0)

Source: Primary Data

Mode of Travel : Another important aspect of Andaman tourism industry is how they reach this lush green islands' paradise from the mainland and to one island from another island. There are only two modes of travel from the mainland to the island and back namely by aircraft and by ships Tourists choose according to their financial budget. Table 7.6 shows the mode of travel used by the tourists at the time of coming to these islands and at the time of going from these islands.

Table 7.6
Modes of Travel / Incoming & Outgoing

Modes of Travel	Number of Respondents/Tourists		
	DT	FT	Total
INCOMING			
By Air	33(45.8) (25.4)	39(54.2) (78.0)	72(100.0) (40.0)
By Ship	97(89.8) (74.6)	11(10.2) (22.0)	108(100.0) (60.0)
Total	130(72.2) (100.0)	50(27.8) (100.0)	180(100.0) (100.0)
OUTGOING			
By Air	42(47.7) (32.3)	46(52.3) (92.0)	88(100.0) (48.9)
By Ship	88(95.7) (67.7)	04(4.3) (8.0)	92(100.0) (51.1)
Total	130(72.2) (100.0)	50(27.8) (100.0)	180(100.0) (100.0)

Source: Primary data.

Table 7.6 shows clearly that majority of the tourists travel by ship of the total sample tourists, 108 tourists representing 60.0% have expressed that they travelled by ship and the remaining 72 representing 40.0% by air. The table also reveals another important fact that majority of the FTs travelled by air. Of the total sample FTs 39 representing 78.0% have travelled by air and the remaining 22% ie. 11 respondents travelled by ship while coming to these islands. But this is reverse in case of DTs. The majority of the DTs choose the ship journey as their mode of travel. Ninety seven representing 74.6% of the total sample DTs have expressed that they travelled by ship and the remaining 25.4% i.e. 33 respondents by air.

As far as the modes of travel, used by the tourists for going from these islands to the mainland is concerned., the table reveals that the number of the tourists who travelled by ship for going out, is less than the number of tourists who travelled by ship for incoming. Of the total tourists, 108(60.0%) respondents travelled by ship while coming into these islands whereas 92 (51.1%) respondents travelled by ship while going to mainland. Even, there is a change in DTs. The reason may me attributed to the fact that those who came by ship might be interested to go by air. But on conversation with the FTs it is understood that they have to choose the airways because of their predetermined programs and the time factor.

Purpose of Visit : The tourism planner hoteliers, organisers, travel agents etc. should understand the motives of the tourists who come to these islands. With the great hard work and by spending a lot of time as the examiner prepares a science question paper for a candidate who has come to write commerce examination, the question paper, the time allotted, paper, material etc., all will be a waste in the same manner, without understanding the purpose of the visit,if the planners, hoteliers etc. plan/organise, there is a lot of chance that these plans/programmes and the efforts may go waste. So understanding the purpose of the visit is very important on the part of the planners/ organsiers. Table 7.7 shows the purpose of the visit of the tourists to these islands.

The table reveals that the main purpose of the visit of tourists to these islands is a pleasure trip and to enjoy the Natural Scenic Beauty of these lush green islands One Hundred and Fifty Four representing 85.6% of the total tourists have expressed the above fact. Among these 154 respondents, 108(83.1%) are DTs and 46(92.0%) are FTs. Eleven out of 180 tourists representing 6.1% have expressed that they came to these islands to explore the business opportunities in these islands and to see the Cellular Jail and the Vipor Island Jail for women. Thirteen (7.2%) out of the total sample consisting of 9(6.9%) DTs and 4(8.0%)FTs have expressed that they visit these islands for academic purpose They belong to the students' category.

Table 7.7
Purpose of the Visit

Purpose	No. of Respondents/Tourists		
	DT	FT	Total
Pleasure Trip & to enjoy the Natural Scenic Beauty	108(70.1) (83.1)	46(29.9) (92.0)	154(100) (85.6)
Business Opportunity	11(100.0) (8.5)	-	11(100.0) (6.1)
Education	9(69.2) (6.9)	4(30.8) (8.0)	13(100.0) (7.2)
Others	2(100.0) (1.5)	– –	2(100.0) (1.1)
Total	130(72.2) (100.0)	50(27.8) (100.0)	180(100) (100.0)

Length of the Stay : Another important point needed to be kept in mind by tourism planners, organisers, etc. is as to how many days the tourists stay or plan to stay in this destination. The more they stay, the more is the income to this place. Table 7.8 shows the length of stay by the tourists in this territory.

Table 7.8
Length of the Stay IN No. of Days

Number of Days	No. of respondents/ Tourists		
	DT	FT	Total
Below 5 days	25(67.6) (19.2)	12(32.4) (24.0)	37(100.0) (20.6)
5 - 10 days	48(60.8) (36.9)	31(39.2) (62.0'	79(100.0) (43.9)
10 - 15 days	36(83.7) (27.7)	7(16.8) (14.0)	43(100.0) (23.9)
15 days & More	21(100.0) (16.2)	- -	21(100.0) (11.6)
Total	130(72.2) (100.0)	50(27.8) (100.0)	180(100.0) (100.0)

Source: Primary data

The above table reveals that the majority of FTs stay upto 10 days in these islands, when compared with the DTs. But at the same time no FTs stay (as per sample) for a period of more than 15 days. But, among DTs, the table has not recorded any significant mark. If the total number of tourists is taken, the tourists stay in these islands upto 15 days. Of the total respondents, 159(88.3%) consists of 109 (83.8) DTs,50(100%) have expressed that their length of stay is from 5-15 days in this Islands. To be more specific, 79 tourists representing 43.9% consist of 48(36.9%) DTs, 31 (62%) FTs said that they would like to stay upto 10 days . Compartively speaking, the length of the stay of tourists, both DTs and FTs, on these islands is on the increase which is a good sign for the development of tourism industry in this territory.

Helping Means of Travel : Table 7.9 is related to the helping means of travel to the tourists, that is, with whose help do they come to these islands? This question is asked with a view to know the actual role of travel agents and tourism office.

Table 7.9
Helping Means of Travel

Helping Means	No of Respodents/ Tourists		
	DT	FT	Total
Own/ Self	112(94.1) (86.2)	7(5.9) (14.0)	119(100.0) (66.1)
Through Tourist Office	18(100.0) (10.0)	6(33.3) (4.6)	12(66.7) (24.0)
Through Travel Agents	12(27.9) (9.2)	31(72.1) (62.0)	43(100.0) (23.9)
Total	130(72.2) (100.0)	50(27.8) (100.0)	180(100.0) (100.0)

Source: Primary Data.

The above table reveals that 119 respondents with 66.1% consisting of 112(86.2%) DTs and (14.0%) FTs said that they reached these islands with their own efforts, 18 respondənts with 10.0% consisting of 6(4.6%) DTs and 12(24%) FTs have expressed that they reached this territory with the help of Tourism Office and 43 tourists with 23.9% consisting of 12(9.2%)DTs and 31(62.0%) FTs have clearly expressed that they came to these islands with the help of travel agents. It is very clear from the table that FTs depend more on the Travel Agents and Tourism Office.

Modes of Transport for Inter-Islands: After having reached Port Blair, the entry gate of A & N Islands, the tourists plan to visit inter islar.ds depending upon their programme. Some tourists may go to inter-islands and some may not. There are only two modes of transport namely by road and by sea Table 7.10 shows the modes of transport used by the tourists to go to inter-island.

Table 7.10
Modes of Transport for Inter-Islands

Transport	No. Of Respondents/Tourists		
	DT	FT	Total
By Boat	41(89.1)	05(10.9)	46(100.0)
	(31.5)	(10.0)	(25.60
By Bus	29(90.6)	03(9.4)	32(100.0)
	(22.3)	(6.0)	(17.8)
By Taxi	07(43.8)	09(56.2)	16(100.0)
	(5.4)	(18.0)	(8.9)
By Private Van/Car	17(80.9)	04(19.1)	21(100.0)
	(13.1)	(8.0)	(11.6)
Did not Go	36(55.4)	29(44.6)	65(100.0)
	(27.7)	(58.0)	(36.1)
Total	130(72.2)	50(27.8)	180(100.0)
	(100.0)	(100.0)	(100.0)

Source : Primary data.

As per the Table 7.10, 115 with 63.9% of the total respondents, consisting of 21(42.0%)FTs and 94 (72.9%)DTs, have reported that they visited inter-islands. The remaining 29(58.O%)FTs and 29 (58.0) FTs and 36(27.7%) DTs have reported that they could not go to inter islands. Tight schedule of their other programmes, fear of going through the Jarawa area, fear of missing flights, etc. are the reasons submitted by them. Of the total sample tourists, 46(25.6%) tourists consisting of 41(31.5%)DTs and 5(10%) FTs used boats, 32(17.8%) tourists consisiting of 29(22.3%) DT and 3(6.0%)FTs used buses, and 37(20.6%) tourists consisting of 24(18%) DT and 13(26.0%) FTs used private taxi, van, car etc. The table clearly reveals that the tourists prefer boat as well as bus as their modes of transport.

Places of Stay : Place of stay is the most important determinant of the length of stay It is the facility of vital importance needed at the destination. In A&N Islands, both the govt. accommodations and private accommodations are available. Table 7.11 gives the particulars of the places of stay.

It is clear from the above table that the majority of the tourists stay in Pvt.accommodation in both the cases of DTs and FTs. One hundred and one sample tourists, representing 56.1% of the total tourists, have expressed that they have chosen private accommodations. It consists of 58(44.6%)DTs and 43 (86.%) FTs. Tourists, staying in Govt. accommodation, were, as per the above table, comparitively less. Only very limited number of tourists i.e 7 (14.0%) FTs and 32 (24.6%) DTs stayed in the govt. accommodation. Eleven tourists in the domestic section stayed with their friends & relatives. This table pictures that the accommodation from the private sector has good prospects in these islands One more point is clear from the table that the FTs have used private accommodation more often than the DTs.

Table 7.11
Places of (Accommodation)

Places of Stay	No. of Respondents/Tourists		
	DT	FT	Total
Government/Municipal			
Accommodation	32(82.1)	07(17.9)	39(100.0)
	(24.6)	(14.0)	(21.7)
Private Accommodation	58(57.4)	43(42.6)	101(100.0)
	(44.6)	(86.0)	(56.1)
With Friends	11(100.0)	-	11.(100.0)
	(8.5)	-	(6.1)
Regional Sangam /			
Association/Club/			
Samajam	29(100.0)	-	29(100.0)
	(22.3)	-	(16.1)
Total	130(72.2)	50(27.8)	180(100.0)
	(100.0)	(100.0)	(100.0)

Source : Primary Data.

VIEWS AND SATISFACTION

The views and satisfaction of the tourists who visit the destination are the basis for the dovelopment of tourism in any destination. After getting some important information from the tourists regarding their place of stay, mode of transport and travel, source of information etc., it is important to know their views and the extent of their satisfaction about the facilities that are available in the A&N islands. The parameters like "YES" or "No" , "Excellent", "Good", "Satisfactory", "Unsatisfactory" and

"No Comment" were used. By using the parameters, the views and satisfaction of the tourists who visited these islands have been obtained, grouped and briefly presented.

About Journey From Mainland : Table 7.12 shows the views and satisfaction of the tourists regarding the comfortable journey they performed from the mainland.

Table 7.12
Views regarding the comfortable Journey

View	No. of Respondents/Tourists DT	FT	Total
No Trouble, Free & Comfortable	21(44.7) (16.2)	26(55.3) (52.0)	47(100.0) (26.1)
Somehow comfortable	7(48.6) (13.1)	18(51.4) (36.0)	35(100.0) (19.4)
Oh! Lot of Trouble & Uncomfortable	92(93.9) (70.7)	06(6.1) (12.0)	98(100.0) (54.5)
Total	130(72.2) (100.0)	50(27.8) (100.0)	180(100.0) (100.0)

Souıce : Primary data.

The above table reveals that 47 respondents indicating, 26.1% of the total sample comprising 26(52.0%)FTs and 21(16.2%) DTs, have happily stated that they had a very comfortable journey; 35 respondents amounting to 19.4% comprising 18(36.0%) FTs and 17(13.1%) DTs have said that their journey was somewhat comfortable but the remaining tourists i.e 98 representing 54.5% consisting of 6(12.0%) FT and 92(70.8%) DTs have painfuly expressed that they had a lot of trouble at the time of journey. Problems in getting the tickets, in the mainland of India, at

Calcutta, at Chennai, at Visakkapatnam unnecessearily getting stranded at these places, no proper guidance at the mainland, non -co-operation on the part of the tourism offices and officers in the mainland, personal problems due to the wastage of time in the mainland are the general problems, expressed by the tourists.

Another analysis from this present table with the Table 7.9 clearly conveys a fact that those tourists, who came to these islands (with the helping means of travel) through the travel agents, had comfortably travelled when they came from mainland. On the other hand, those who came on their own (self help) had travelled in somewhat discomfort. This table leaves a fact that the travel agents have very good prospects in these islands.

Level of Statisfactoin About Transport : Next to the comfortable or uncomfortable journey, their level of satisfaction about the transport from the mainland-island,and island - island transport was obtained. Table 7.13 related to the level of satisfaction about the transport between Mainland-Island-Mainland and Table 7.14 is related to the satisfaction about the Island-Island transport.

Table 7.13

Level of satisfaction about Mainland -Island Transport

Level of Satisfaction	No. of Respondents/Tourists		
	DT	FTs	Total
Excellent	28(49.1)	29(50.9)	57(100.0)
	(21.5)	(58.0)	(31.)
Good	33(76.8)	10(23.2)	43(100.0)
	(25.4)	(20.0)	(23.9)
Satisfactory	29(76.3)	9(23.7)	38(100.0)
	(22.3)	(18.0)	(21.1)
Unsatisfactory	32(94.1)	2(5.9)	34(100.0)

	(24.6)	(4.0)	(18.8)
No Comment	8(100.0)	–	8(100.0)
	(6.2)		(4.5)
Total	130(72.2)	50(27.8)	180(100.0)
	(100.0)	(100.0)	(100.0)

Source: Primary data.

Table 7.14

Level of Satisfaction about the Island-Island Transport

Level of Satisfaction	No. Of Respondents/Tourists		
	DT	FT	Total
Excellent	19(90.5)	2(9.5)	21(100.0)
	(14.6)	(4.0)	(11.7)
Good	21(84.0)	4(16.0)	25(100.0)
	(16.2)	(8.0)	(13.9)
Satisfactory	15(53.6)	13(46.4)	28(100.0)
	(11.5)	(26.0)	(15.6)
Unsatisfactory	39(95.1)	2(4.9)	41(100.0)
	(30.0)	(4.0)	(22.7)
Did not visit Inter Islands	36(55.4)	29(44.6)	65(100.0)
	(27.7)	(58.0)	(36.1)
Total	130(72.2)	50(27.8)	180(100.0)
	(100.0)	(100.0)	(100.0)

Source: Primary data

Table 7.13 reveals that majority of the tourists have good opinion about the transport by which they travelled from the mainland. It is seen from the table that 57 tourists(31.7%) expressed that their satisfaction was excellent. It includes

29(58%) FTs and 28(21.5%) DTs 43 Tourists(23.9%) said that their level of satisfaction is Good. It includesl0(20.0%) FTs and 33(25.4%) DTs. 38 tourists expressed their level of satisfaction as "Unsatisfactory" and 8 tourists did not give any comment on the level of satisfaction. Another fact comes to the for when linking this table with the Table 7.6. That is, those tourists, who expressed their level of satisfaction as excellent & good, are the ones who have travelled by air; and those who called it as good, satisfactory and unsatisfactory are all who travelled by ship. So it is clear from these tables that the shipping transport facilities should be increased in order to raise the level of satisfaction.

From the Table 7.14 it is clear that only about 2/3rd of the tourists visit inter-islands. This is more acute in case of FTs. Sixty five representing 36.1% of the total respondents consisting of 29(58.0%) FTs and 36(27.7%) DTs did not visit inter islands. Forty one(22.8%) consisting of 39(30.0%) DTs and 2(4.0%) FTs have expressed that their level of satisfaction as "Unsatisfactory". Only the remaining the respondents have expressed it as "Good", "Satisfactory" and "Excellent". From this table it is clear that the inter-island transport needs to be improved to attract more tourists.

Views About Accommodation : Next to the views and levels of satisfaction of tourists about transport, tourists' views and satisfaction about the accommodation is necessary /important from the point of view of the hoteliers, A & N Administration, Private lodge owners, etc. The views and satisfaction are the only opportunity and basis to them to improve the accommodation facilities at least to understand the status of their accommodation. Table 7.15 gives the views of the tourists about the accommodation

Table 7.15
Views of Tourists about the Accomodation

Views	No of Respondents/Tourists		
	DT	FT	Total
No Problem, Free & Comfortable	30(73.2) (23.1)	11(26.8) (22.0)	41(100.0) (22.5)
Somewhat Comfortable	22(36.1) (16.9)	39(63.9) (78.0)	61(100.0) (22.9)
Oh.! Lot of Problems	38(100.0) (29.2)	- (21.1)	38(100.0)
No Comment	40(100.0) (30.8)	-	40(100.0) (22.2)
Total 180(100.0)	130(72.2) (100.0)	50(27.8) (100.0)	(100.0)

Source: Primary Data

The above table reveals that 38 respondents representing 21.1% of the total sample have expressed that they had a lot of problems in getting accommodation. All are the Domestic Tourists. 40 tourists did not give any comment about the accommodation. Of the total sample, 41(22.8%) consisiting of 30(23.1%) DTs and 11(22.0%) FTs have expressed that they were very comfortable and they did not face any problem in the accommodation whereas 61 tourists consisting of 22 DTs and 39 FTs said half heartedly that they were somewhat comfortable. No cleanliness, no hygienic conditions, power problems water problems, unsatisfactory service, too much of distance from the bus terminus, taxi stand and comparatively too much of rent are some of the views expressed by the tourists

Level of Satisfaction : Table 7.16 is related to the level of satisfaction about the accommodation facility in these islands. Accommodation facility is the primary facility to be provided to the tourists in order to develop the tourism industry in this territory.

Table 7.16
Level of Satisfaction about the Accommodation

Level	No. of Respondents/Tourists		
	DT	FT	Total
Excellent	30(73.2)	11(26.8)	41(100.0)
	(23.1)	(22.0)	(22.8)
Good	11(44.0)	14(56.0)	25(100.0)
	(8.5)	(28.0)	(13.9)
Satisfactory	31(79.5)	08(20.5)	39(100.0)
	(23.8)	(16.0)	(21.7)
Unsatisfactory	18(51.4)	17(48.6)	35(100.0)
	(13.8)	(34.0)	(19.4)
No Comment	40(100.0)	-	40(100.0)
	(30.8)		(22.2)
Total	130(72.2)	50(27.8)	180(100.0)
	(100.0)	(100.0)	(100.0)

Source: Primary data.

Of the total respondents, 41 representing 22.8%- consisting of 30(23.1%) DTs and 11(22.0%) FTs expressed their level of satisfaction as "Excellent ; 25 representing 13.9 consisting of 11(8.5%) DTs and 14(28.0%) FTs expressed it as good; 39 representing 21.7% comprising 31(23.9%) DTs and 8(16.0%) FTs expressed it as satisfactory; 35(19.4%) including 18(13.8%) DTs and 17(34.0%) FTs expressed their level of satisfaction as unsatisfactory and 40(22.2%) tourists consisting of only DTs did not give any reply.

About Food : Food is the important basic facility besides accommodation. This is required by the tourists not only at the Port Blair but also during the travel to other places particularly to the JollyBouy, Redskin, Cinque Island. Radha Nagar Beach, Lalji Beach, etc. These places are mentioned because, in these places, the provision for food/food facilily is totally absent. Table 7.17 shows the places where the tourists eat their delicious food.

Table 7.17
Eating Places For Tourists

Places	No of Resnondents/ Tourists		
	DT	FT	Total
At the Place where they stay	47 (55.3)	38(44.7)	85(100.0)
	(36.2)	(76.0)	(47.2)
Outside the place of stay	63(88.7)	8(11.3)	71(100.0)
	(48.5)	(16.0)	(39.0)
Anywhere	20(83.3)	4(16.7)	24(100.0)
	(15.3)	(8.0)	13.4)
Total	130(72.2)	50(27.8)	180(100.0)
	(100.0)	(100.0)	(100.0)

Source: Primary data

It is evident from the Table 7.17 that, of the total tourists, 85 representing 47.2% take their food in the places where they stay. It includes 47 (36.2%) DTs and 38 (76.0%) FTs. 95 tourists representing 52.8% including 63 (48.5%) DTs and 8 (16.0%) FTs take their food outside the place of stay and they don't take it at the place where they stay. It is also evident from the table that the Tourists prefer to have their food only at the place where they stay. Table 7.18 shows the level of satisfaction of the tourists about the hotels, or the places where they take their food.

Table 7.18
Level of Satisfaction about the Food & Hotels

Level of Satisfaction	No. of Respondents/Tourists		
	DT	FT	Total
Excellent	14 (10.8)	9 (18.0)	23 (12.8)
Good	21 (16.2)	11 (22.0)	32 (17.8)
Satisfactory	29 (22.3)	13 (26.0)	42 (23.3)
Unsatisfactory	61 (46.9)	17 (34.0)	78 (43.3)
No Comment	5 (3.8)	– –	5 (2.8)
Total	130(72.2) (100.0)	50(27.8) (100.0)	180(100.0) (100.0)

Source: Primary data

The Table clearly shows that the majority of the tourists are of the opinion that the food facility offered by the destination i.e A&N islands is unsatisfactory. Of the total sample, 78 representing 43.3% including 61(46.9%) DTs and 17(34.0%) FTs have expressed their level of satisfaction as Unsatisfactory. Though 5 Tourists have made no comment, only 23 tourists representing 12.8% including 14(7.8%) DTs and 9(18.0%) FTs have rated their satisfaction to the level of "Excellent". The main facts of this table are that the facility for the food should be increased, and such facilities should be made available at all the places of tourist interest. Poor waiter services, language problems in the hotels, less variety of food, of tastes etc. are the reasons, for their dissatisfaction, expressed at the time of the interview with them.

About Bar : Bar facility is another important supporting factor to the development of this Industry. Some tourists may not even like the existence of this facility. They do not want to see that others drink. On the contrary, some may not prefer a particular place/destination if such bar facility is not available so it is considered as one of the important parts of the tourist products. Table 7.19 shows the views of the tourists regarding the Bar facility provided in these islands.

Table 7.19
Views of the Tourists about Bar facilily

Views	No. of Respondents/Tourists		
	DT	FT	Total
Excellent	9(81.8) (6.9)	2(18.2) (4.0)	11(100.0) (6.1)
Good	12(60.0) (9.2)	8(40.0) (16.0)	20(100.0) (11.1)
Satisfactory	51(70.8) (39.2)	21(29.2) (42.0)	72(100.0) (40.0)
Unsatisfactory	37(66.1) (28.5)	19(33.9) (38.0)	56(100.0) (31.1)
Should be avoided	21(100.0) (16.2)	-	21(100.0) (11.7)
Total	130(72.2) (100.0)	50(27.8) (100.0)	180(100.0) (100.0)

Source: Primary Data

It is evident from the table that all the foreign tourists consume liquor and they do expect that the bar facility should be one of the prerequisites of the tourism industry, whereas some of the DTs do not like this facility at all. Though very little number of respondents expressed their level of satisfaction as "Excellent" , 72(40.0%) respondents including 51(39.2%) DTs and 21(42.0%) FTs expressed it as satisfactory and 56(31.1%) respondents including 37(28. 5%) DTs and 19(38.0%) FTs have very painfully expressed their level of satisfaction as Unsatisfactory. But all the consuming tourists have reported that only the city has the Bar facility and the inter islands do not have such facility and hence going to inter-islands is to be decided by giving it a second thought

About Price Level : In order to understand their feelings about the prices prevailing in these islands for food, transport, taxi, conducted tours, accommodation etc., question was asked regarding the same. Uniformly all the tourists are of the opinion that the flight fare is too much and just can not be tolerable. As far as the other items are concerned they give different ratings of their feelings and these are summarised and presented in a table form. Table 7.20 shows the views about the price level in A & N islands.

Table 7.20
Views about the Price Level

View/Rating	No. of Respondents/Tourists		
	DT	FT	Total
Very High	78(78.8)	21(21.2)	99(100.0)
	(60.0)	(42.0)	(55.0)
High	12(46.2)	14(53.8)	26(100.0)
	(9.2)	(28.0)	(14.5)
Tolerable	5(62.5)	3(37.5)	8(100.0)
	(3.9)	(6.0)	(4.4)
More or Less			
Equal to Mainland	7(38.9)	11(61.1)	18(100.0)
	(5.4)	(22.0)	(10.0)
Cheap	28(96.6)	1(3.4)	29(100.0)
	(21.5)	(2.0)	(16.1)
Total	130(72.2)	50(27.8)	180(100.0)
	(100.0)	(100.0)	(100.0)

Source: Primary Data.

As per the table, it is very clear that the price levels in this distination are felt by the majority of the tourists as very high & high. Of the total sample, 125 tourists representing about 70.0% including 90 (69.2%) DTs and 35(70.%) FTs have stated that the prices are very high when compared with the mainland. So they felt " why should we carry from here an extra luggage". They are pointing out each and every item starting from shopping to food. This table gives a fact that the price control system is to be introduced with an efficient supervision.

About Tourism Attractions : Tourist attractions are the magnets of the Tourims Industry through which the tourists are attracted. Tourism attractions have been discussed in the Chapter IV. Natural Scenic Beauty, Social, Cultural & Religious aspects etc. are the important ingredients of the tourism attractions. Understanding the level of satisfaction and the view of the tourists about the tourism attractions is very important from the point of view of the development of the industry. Table 7.21 shows the views and the level of satisfaction of the tourists about the tourism attractions.

The table clearly pictures the resourcefulness of these islands for the Tourism Industry. As far as the FTs are concerned, almost all the respondents expressed their level of satisfaction as "Excellent". The FTs were of the opinion at the time of the discussion with them after getting the filled up questionnaires, that they are much impressed by the social and cultural aspects of these islands. They expressed that this land is considered as a Heaven, Paradise and what not... is only because of the unity among the people from different cultures, religions, region etc. This land is not known to all, they added.

As far as the DTs are concerned, of the total sample, 112(86.2%) expressed their satisfaction as " excellent" about Natural Scenic Beauty, 98 with 75.4% expressed as excellent about Social aspects and so on. The important point to be noted is that none of the DTs has expressed as

Table 7.21
Views and Levels of Satisfaction About Tourism Attractions

Views & Levels/Attraction	No. of Respondents / Tourists & Rating			
	Excellent	Good	Satisfactory	Unsatisfactory
DOMESTIC TOURIST				
1. Natural Scenic Beauty	112(86.2)	13(10.0)	5(3.8)	-
2. Social Aspects	98(75.4)	22(16.9)	10(7.7)	-
3. Cultural Aspects	102(78.5)	25(19.2)	3(2.3)	-
4. Religious Aspects	89(68.5)	5(3.8)	16(12.3)	20(15.4)
5. Places of Interests	121(93.1)	9(6.9)	-	-
6. Local Sight Seeing	99(76.2)	21(61.1)	10(7.7)	-
FOREIGN TOURISTS				
1. Natural Scenic Beauty	48(96.0)	2 (4.0)	-	-
2. Social Aspects	50(100.0)	-	-	-
3. Cultural Aspects	50(100.0)	-	-	-
4. Religious Aspects	46(92.0)	4 (8.0)	-	-
5. Places of Interests	50(100.0)	-	-	-
6. Local sight seeing	50(100.0)	-	-	-

Source : Primary Data-% is calculated on the total number of DTs and FTs respectively.

'Unsatisfactory' as regards all the attractions except religious aspect. 20 tourists representing 15.4% expressed that they are not satisfied with the religious aspects of the A & N islands.This table clearly conveys to all the planners, officials, tour operators, travel agents, nation lovers, departments hoteliers, researchers, academicians, etc. that the tourism in A & N islands has a potential prospect of a very high degree particularly the FTs can be attracted and hence they can plan for rich tourism in these islands.

About Supporting Facilities : After having analysed the views and levels of satisfaction of the tourists about the essential facilities, the views of the tourists about the supporting facilities have also been analysed and presented in the Table 7.22.

Table 7.22
Views and Satisfaction about the Supporting Facilites

Supporting Facilities	No. of Respondents/Tourists Expressed as Excellent	Good	Satisfactory	Unsatis-factory	Total
DOMESTIC TOURISTS					
1. Banking Services	38(29.2)	49(37.7)	31(23.8)	12(9.2)	130(100)
2. Postal Services	22(16.9)	24(18.5)	26(20.0)	58(44.6)	130(100)
3.Telecommunications	93(71.5)	19(14.6)	08(6.2)	-	130(100)
4. Health Services	26(20.0)	24(18.5)	19(14.6)	87(66.9)	130(100)
5 Shopping	23(17.7)	49(37.7)	31(23.8)	27(20.8)	130(100)
6. Traffic Sevices	122(93.8)	08(6.2)	—	—	130(100)
7. Photographers	94(72.3)	36(27.7)	—	—	130(100)
8. Libraries	22(16.9)	14(10.8)	16(12.3)	78(12.3)	130(100)
9. Books/Peridocials	21(16.2)	13(10.0)	17(13.1)	79(60.7)	130(100)
10. Personal Safety	72(55.4)	48(36.9)	10(7.7)	—	130(100)
11. Law & Order Assistance	122(93.8)	8(6.2)	—	—	130(100)
12. Service of Tourism Dept)	39(30.0)	50(38.5)	30(23.1)	11(8.5)	130(100
13. Tourist Guides	04(3.1)	13(10.0)	21(16.2)	92(70.7)	130(100)
14. Cinema & Other Recreation	08(6.2)	22(16.9)	2(1.5)	98(75.4)	130(100)
15. Aiding facilities at the place of Coral Islands.	87(66.9)	18(13.8)	17(13.1)	08(6.2)	130(100)
FOREIGN TOURISTS					
Banking Service	—	—	—	—	—
Postal Service	—	—	—	—	—
Telecommunications	36(72.0)	13(26.0)	—	1(2.0)	50(100)
Health Services	—	28(56.0)	9(18.0)	13(26.0)	50(100)
Shopping	46(92.0)	4(8.0)	—	—	50(100)
Traffic Services	39(78.0)	11(22.0)	—	—	50(100)
Photographers	33(66.0)	17(34.0)	—	—	50(100)
Libraries	27(54.0)	12(24.0)	11(22.0)	—	50(100)
Books/Peridocials	—	—	—	—	—
Personal Safety	47(94.0)	3(6.0)	—	—	50(100)
Law&Order Assistantce	—	—	—	—	—
Service of Tourists Dept	31(62.0)	16(32.0)	Nocomment	3(6.0)	50(100)

Tourists Guides	—	—	6(12.0)	44(88.0)	50(100)
Cinema&Other	33(66.0)	17(34.0)	—	50(100)	
Recreation	No Comment				
Aiding Facilities at theplace of Coral Islands	39(78.0)	11(22.0)	—	—	50(100)

Sources : Primary Data.

The above table reveals that the majority of the DTs as well as FTs are happy with the supporting facilities, provided by this destination. The FTs are not happy with the Health service because 13 FTs representing 26.0% have expressed that the services are unsatisfactory to them. But both the FTs and DTs expressed that the facility of provision for tourist guide is also unsatisfactory. Except these facilities, the remaining facilities fully attract the tourists.

The information, analysed above, provides an insight into the tourism industry and the views of the tourists, level of satisfaction of the tourists about the tourism facilities provided by this destination i.e A & N islands. It also furnishes some important information about the tourists who normally visit these islands i.e their age, sex, income, occupational aspects etc. and some other information about the purpose of their visit, preference of choices, idea about the attractions, source of information, helping means of travel, quality of food they like, expected services etc. All this information is very much useful to elicit the problems facing the tourism industry in these islands, to make out a policy suitable to these islands to promote the tourism industry in A & N islands. The analysed information will be very much helpful to all the planners, hoteliers, researchers, govt. authorities, tour operator and those who are interested in tourism for further improvement in the total facilities, to be provided to the tourists, on which the ultimate success of the tourism industry of A & N islands will depend.

8

PROBLEMS OF TOURISM

The problems of the tourism industry are the basis for the action plans of the authorities Based on the survey, analysis of the views of the tourists, discussion with the tourists, personal visits of the important beaches, roads, places etc., informal discussion with the offices and officials, local people etc., some problems facing the tourism industry have been identified. There are some common problems due to the inadequate infrastructural facilities facing the tourism industry as a whole. Also, the tourists, both Indian as well as foreign, who visited these islands, faced a number of problems and difficulties while undertaking their travel / journey to and in these islands. Among them the major problems have been discussed and presented below under the following headings

ACCOMMODATION AND CATERING

Providing accommodation and good catering is the foremost function of tourism department, hotels, lodge owners etc. in order to attract more number of tourists. But most of the accommodations do not have proper catering facility. Some guest houses provide canteen facility but they charge exorbitant prices for the meals. This problem is more acute in inter islands. So the tourists are compelled to take food from outside the lodges where they stay. Since the cost of ship journey is comparitively acceptable, at the arrival of ships there are a large number of tourists. At the time of large arrivals, the tourists find it difficult to get accommodation and food and it creates frustration among them. Non-availability of accustomed food (rice for South Indian and rotti for North Indian and the like) is another problem.

Mojor number of the lodges and accommodations are situated only in the Port Blair city. A large number of tourists, wishing to visit other islands, face a lot of problems for getting accommodation for the night and they have to come back on any account to Port Blair. Tourists who go to places like Wandoor, JollyBouy, Redskin etc. face difficulties to get proper food in respective places. Of the fifty foreign tourists, 39 (78.0%) and 130 domestic tourists 22 (16.9%) expressed their level of satisfaction about accommodation as some what comfortable. 38 (29.2%) domestic tourists expressed that they faced a lot of problems. As far as the food is concerned, 78 tourists representing 43.3% of the sample expressed their satisfaction as "Unsatisfactory". Most of the lodges do not have laundry, protected drinking water, proper ventilation, laboratory, mosquito net facilities and these lodges are in unhygienic conditions. Many of the sophisticated foreign tourists and the rich visitors feel that there is no chance to spend their money to their level of satisfaction due to the lack of luxurious star hotels.

TRANSPORT

There are two kinds of transport problems, faced by the tourists arriving at Port Blair, the problems related to the transport between the Mainland and the Islands and the problems related to the Inter-Islands transport. As far as the former case is concerned, non-availability of tickets for both flights as well as ships, high cost of transport and wastage of time are the general problems of the tourists. The tourists can not plan according to their own convenience because it would never suit the shipping programme and the availability of tickets. Out of the total sample, 98 tourists including 92 domestic tourists and 6 foreign tourists have expressed that they faced intolerable problems due to the above reasons, and 34 tourists said that they are dissatisfied.

SHIP MANAGEMENT

There is no proper control, facility etc. inside the ships. Such inefficient management adds fuel to the transport problems. The result is that the bunk passengers continuously use the toilets and bathrooms meant for the cabin class passengers. These activities of the bunk passengers create frustration in the minds of tourists.

PASSENGER WAITING HALL

Lack of passenger waiting hall at the mainland ports is another frustrating problem. The author witnessed three times at the Chennai Port, the passengers running from one place to another to take shelter when there it was raining. Finally some went into the Shipping Corporation of India's godown and some stood under the crane engine. Most of the luggage kept lying in the open yard and in the rain. There is no guest house facility near the harbours in the mainland.

GETTING TICKETS

This is another problem. At present the tickets are reserved in Port Blair. Tourists have to contact the SCI or the Directorate of Shipping of the A & N Administration situated in the mainland for the reservation of tickets. In this process, the comunication gap plays an adverse role.

ENTERTAINMENT AND RECREATION

As far as the entertainment and recreational facilities are concerned, the Television, Radio, Video and Cable connections, provided by the hotels, are comparitively less.

It is found that majority of the hotels, due to their smallness in size, do not provide all entertainment and recreational facilities. Only very few hotels provide such facility.

SEWAGE DISPOSAL

Tourists come to these islands with high expectations. At the moment they arrive at Port Blair, they feel disgusted when they cross the loathsome sewage spots, cowdung on the mainroads, pan spits, coconut waste, dirty insects' resorts, harmful garbage etc. Some senseless persons throw wastes, empty bottles, bodies of the dead animals, empty packages into gutters which results in the blocking of sewage. All this spoils the beauty of the beautiful islands.

LIGHTING FACILITY

Carbyn's Cove, Wandoor, Chidiatappu are some of the best beaches around Port Blair. Besides these beaches, Havelock, Car Nicobar, Campbell Bay also have good beaches. Of all the beaches, only Carbyn's Cove, the Channai Marina of Port Blair, has lighting facility. But there is no lighting facility for the roads which go to Carbyin's Cove beach. The same is the case with the other beaches also. Those tourists, who want to enjoy sea breeze at night, are unable to stay at the beach after 5.30 pm due to lack of lighting facility. Due to this problem and lack of security facility, some immoral activities on some tourists are witnessed.

MAINTENANCE

Particularly the beaches are not properly maintained and developed. The beaches are dressed with empty liquor bottles, cowdungs, rotten animal bodies, harmful stones and broken timbers with some iron nails, waste of coconut trees etc. Some people, residing near the shore or beach, use the beauty beach for their open toilet purposes. So the tourists find it very difficult to locate a place in the beaches to sit and gossip, converse and chit chat.. There is no seating arrangment in the beaches.

SHOPPING COMPLEX

The A&N islands is industrially backward area. Economically, it is still at the infant stage. Only very recently, the Port Blair City is becoming famous for shell crafts and other handicraft products. It is felt by the majority of the tourists that these handicrafts products are quoted at extrordinary high price. To regulate the flow and prices of such products, in A&N Islands, there is no fair price shop or shopping complex. Twenty seven tourists expressed that they are not satisfied with the shopping facilities available in the A&N islands.

PUBLIC TOILETS

For the healthy tourism, the quality of the physical environment is the basis for attracting the tourists. The surroundings are very essential for this tourism industry becasue it attracts tourists through their outstanding beauty and recreational facilities Public toilet facility is totally absent in the important beaches like Carbyn's Cove, Wandoor etc. Very recently, the A&N Administration has constructed some public toilets at very important places and that too when some of them are kept closed and the majority of them do not function at all. There is no 'pay and use' toilet unit in these islands. Especially during the temple festivals, govt. celebrations etc. the people gather at one place i.e the places where the celebrations and festivals are organised. The people use the public places as their open toilet which causes heavy damages to the beauty of the sea shore, road side, public grounds like Gymkhana ground, Netaji Ground etc., and the quality of environment. Hence, the need for public toilets is many times greater than the existing facility. At present, the beaches, particularly Carbyn's Cove, are also used for fishing and due to this careless management the shores and beaches get heavily polluted.

BUS TERMINUS

Port Blair has only one bus terminus situated at Aberdeen Bazar. There is no taxi stand anywhere in these islands. The existing bus terminus is not comfortable to the travellers due to the lack of adequate waiting hall or other shelter facilities. The present bus terminus is seen always crowded. There is no display of the bus timings and no systematic control and announcements of bus departure time. The author himself witnessed many times that the passengers were greatly vexed and worried by frequently changing the buses before the departure time. Person at the enquiry counter is hardly seen by the passengers.

LANGUAGE

A & N islands is a miniature India. People from different parts of India live on these islands. About 33 languages are being spoken on these islands. But the business sector is dominated by the Tamilians and Panjabies. Tourists coming from different parts of India and abroad to the A&N islands face language problem.

ENTERTAINMENT OUTSIDE THE STAY

Entertainment facilities are less in the Port Blair city and are absolutely absent in the inter-islands. There are only 5 theatres in these islands and that too all the theatres are situated in the Port Blair city. Tourists do not enjoy the cinemas screened in these theatres becasue they might have already seen these films not less than atleast one year before in the mainland. The following are the main things absent in this territory.

1. Acquarium
2. Exhibition Hall
3. Fresh water swimming pool
4. Museum

5. Rope ways
6. Cinema theatres in the inter-islands

LACK OF ROPEWAYS AND LIFTS

Here in A&N islands, the ropeways is absolutely absent though it could be easily made for which there are a lot of pointing points available. Almost all the tourists expressed that the absence of ropeways is a great handicap to the tourism of A&N Islands.

DURING SUMMER VACATION

All schools and colleges under this A&N Administration have their summer vacation during the months of May, June and July of every year. So the reservation of tickets for both ships and flights starts from the month of January onwards to go from A&N islands to mainland and from the month of April onwards to come to A&N islands from the mainland. During this period, though it is an off season for the tourism, getting tickets to go to and come from the mainland is really a problem for the tourists. Unnecessary blocking of the tickets in the air reservation and the ship reservation by the influential persons adds fuel to the burning problem. Many tourists expressed that they could not go to the mainland due to the teachers' sailing etc.

LESS DEVELOPED PLACES

Generally, the places developed in these islands for the purpose of tourism are very few. Again, quantum of development of these places is also less. Places like Gymkana Ground, Marina Park, Wandoor Beach, Chidiatappu Sand Beach, Radhanagar Beach, Lalgi Beach, Carbyn's Cove Beach, way to the Carbyn's Cove Beach can very well be developed to the fullest satisfaction of the tourists.

ABSENCE OF FOLK DANCE TOURS

A & N islands is a peculier place containing all types of people i.e from all regions of our India, aborigins of these islands. Folk dances of each region and aborigin like Jarawas, Onges, Nicobarese etc. could very well be arranged and developed in order to promote tourism. But such dances are totally absent in the area of tourism. Tourists, by comparing the Goa folk dance tourism/tours, eagerly asked about the folk dance tours.

TOURIST GUIDES

Availability of Tourist Guides in A & N islands is another problem. The Govt. of India Tourist Office, located in Junglighat, has been giving training to the candidates. But the very unhappy news is that no one shows much interest in such courses. Hence, they could arrrange for only 7 tourists guides. The rates, fixed by the Govt. of India, Tourist Office is comparitively higher and hence, the hoteliers are reluctant (little bit) to hire the services of the tourist guides. Moreover, they are engaged in some other jobs. So their availability at the time of their requirement is also doubtful and hence the tourists face a lot of problmes.

POSTAL SERVICES

The way the postal department functions is another problem to the tourism sector. The A&N islands has only one Head Post Office with some other branch offices. But the Head Post Office works like any other government department. The office is opened in time i.e at 9.00 hrs. and closes at 16.30 hrs. This territory is not like mainland where always train services and bus services are available. Here people believe in only the air service for their quick means of communication. But the Head Post Office functions like the mainland offices. So the tourists find it very difficult to post letters Registered, Insured etc. on all public holidays and Sundays and even for Saraswathi Puja the Head Post Office is closed.

MILE STONES AND PILLARS

Mile-stones, Sign posts and Name plates are the best friends for new visitors to any place. These are totally absent in this territory. If there is any important minister's visit to these islands, one can see some name boards, made out of wooden plates, for a period of one or two days or at the maximum of ten days and then they stay at the mercy of white ants and the rain. After that it disappears for ever. Due to the lack of concrete mile pillars and sign posts in these islands, it is not possible for the tourists to calculate the kilometres run and to be run.

WATER

The A & N islands receive an average annual rainfall of little more than 3000 mm. The rainfall, received from both the southwest and north east monsoons, is spread over a period of 6 to 7 months. During the next four months (summer season) the rain fall is scanty and there is an acute shortage of water supply even for drinking purpose. At present there is one water storage tank in A&N islands called Dhanikhari Tank. During the summer season tourists find it difficult to take bath. Most of the beaches lack the supply of soft water facility. Almost all the tourists take bath in the sea water but there is no facility for them to take bath in the soft water after that. Even common 'pay and use' bathing facility is not available on these islands. However, in the Carbyn's Cove beach, soft water is provided but water comes at tortoise speed, full of dirt and small insects. It is in open area. So ladies can not take bath by using the tap water. Since it is in the open area and there is a long queue to take bath in the soft water. Sometimes, water is not available through out the day.

OTHER PROBLEMS

Besides the above problems, there are other problems like parking problem, problems due to the narrow roads, one or two theft cases, low payment in the hotels to their employees, absence of publicity, high rate of taxi fares, Lack of pertol pumps in the other islands like Rangat, Mayabunder, Diglipur, Katchal etc., lack of helicopter services to the inter-islands, lack of rail transport, lack of foreign exchange facility in all the banks etc. worry the tourism industry of A&N islands.

After studying and identifying the problems of the tourism in A & N islands, it is very clear that the tourism promotion is yet to attract the attention of the policy makers, planners, hoteliers, researchers, authorities of A&N Administration, Govt. of India etc. to develop this industry in these far flung islands. Though this potential territory has a number of tourism resources, the tourism, the smokeless industry and eco-friendly industry has not been fully taken care of. Hence, it is necessary to offer some valuable suggestions for the tourism planning, tourism development and to promote tourism in the context of environmental protection and its conservation in the A&N islands by taking its carrying capacity and other sensitive issues

9

SUGGESTIONS FOR PLANNING TOURISM

In the previous chapters, a profile about A & N islands, population characteristics, resources, tourism attractions, tourism facilities, places of interest and their features, social, cultural, religious and economic aspects, transport and communication, food, supporting facilities, analysis of data on tourism, growth of tourism in this territory, views and satisfaction of the tourists have been discussed. Each and every aspect of analysation, of discussion, of data is very much useful for the tourists, tour operators, travel agents, tourism organisation, hoteliers, A & N Administration, all govt. officials, researchers, academicians and those who are interested in tourism. After making such a detailed study, how the infant industry tourism could be developed is to be decided and analysed. So in this chapter, full attention is concentrated carefully on planning tourism and its overall development in these islands and hence suggestions for the planning are offered under the various headings.

TYPE OF TOURISM

The first and foremost point to be decided is as to what type of tourism is to be encouraged in these islands. Generally, tourism is classified into Domestic and Foreign. But the classification to be made here is whether rich tourism or cheap tourism. If rich tourism is encouraged, normally, the number of tourists will be less. Income from the tourism industry will considerably increase because the tourists will spend a lot and they would not disturb the normal tradition of these islands. The overall supervision will also be easier. But, whether these islands get always such rich tourism in the long run is the only threat to such rich tourism. Instead, if the cheap tourism is encouraged, more number of tourists will visit these islands. Income from the tourism industry will increase but compartively at less rate because the tourists will spend less. There are possiblities that the socio-cultural tradition of these islands may be disturbed. Then the growth of such cheap tourism must immediately be checked when it begins to damage the original environment or social life of the people of these islands. The carrying capacity of this territory is to be considered while deciding which type of tourism is to be encouraged. It is evident from the tables and discussions in the previous chapters, that the average length of stay is only 7 - 10 days. So the inflow and outflow of tourists are balanced and hence the carrying capacity of these islands is never disturbed. The prediction here is that the cheap tourism will not always be cheap and it is fully hoped that it will not further go to a level of cheaper and the cheapest. So the planning for tourism should be carried out in such a way that all types of tourists, rich or cheap are to be attracted and they should be induced to spend the maximum according to their level of income. The facilities are to be provided in such a way that they will suit all types of tourists inclusive of a satisfactory profit. For example, Mr. A, a rich tourist and Mr.B, an economy class tourist visit A & N islands. A would like to spend more and B less. Mr. A & Mr. B are going for shopping and they would like to buy shell made item with the idea(A) to spend more and with the idea (B) to spend less. Suppose they wish to buy 'Necklace', the island should make available the necklace at the cost of Rs. 1000 per piece which will be preferred by Mr. A with the best quality flaw material and produced by the skilled labour and also another necklace at the cost of Rs. 500 which will suit 'B' with good quality raw material. Otherwise a separate shopping complex with the facilities of "Seconds" may be provided so that the economy call tourists may purchase at less cost. Hence, the restrictions on tourism, i.e. only rich tourists will be allowed and the cheap tourists will not be allowed to visit these islands, need not be imposed at least at the present stage since the tourism Industry in A & N islands is at its infant stage. All tourists are to be encouraged with careful planning.

RESOURCE PLANNING

Planning for tourism development is not an overnight work and that too for sensitive places like A & N islands. All aspects are to be carefully studied and taken into consideration at the time of planning for tourism. Success or failure of the tourism depends fully on how we plan and carefully implement it. While planning, one should not forget that the tourists are the guests who would be dicouraged even if there is a small negligence on the part of the planners. It is a very sensitive issue because a dissatisfied tourist would become the worst advertiser and a turndown friend who would make the industry sick within no time. At the same time, the natural and man made resources should be protected, conserved and should not be damaged. The socio-cultural aspects should not be polluted, damaged and they should also be fully protected and guarded and maintained in such a way the tourists should learn and assimilate the valuable culture of A & N islands.

A & N islands is rich in her resources, particularly tourism resources. All are unexploited, unpolluted and underexploited. Some are studied, enumerated and the rest majority of them are not enumerated and left as they are. 86% of the total area is fully covered with different types of forests by exposing her natural scenic beauty and attracting tourists. Here, people from different regions, religions, different faiths have been living without any difference of opinion. There are good prospects for the tourism but at the same time, growth of this tourism industry should not affect the environment, pollute the socio-cultural life style of the people of these islands. So effective care must be taken at the time of making plans for the development of tourism in these islands. The tourism resources are to be planned and presented to the tourists in such a way that more and more number of tourists both foreign and domestic tourists are attracted to these islands without affecting the life style of the people of these islands. Hence the experts, academicians and specialists from the different fields are to be called and consulted and the planning for tourism is to be made.

ACCOMMODATION

While planning for tourism, what kind of accommodation to be provided to the different types of tourists must be decided. For this purpose, the status of the tourists, income level of the tourists, their possible programmes, pattern of expenditure, foreign or domestic etc., are to be taken into account. Number of hotels which will accommodate the rich tourists are found only in Port Blair city, but the inter-islands do not have such accommodation facility. At the same time, even in Port Blair, the accommodation which may facilitate the stay for middle class or lower class tourists is not enough and totally absent in the inter- islands where the tourists have to fully depend upon the PWD or Forest department guest houses. If any officer is on tour to the other island the possiblity of getting accommodation in such guest houses for the tourists will be nil. Tourists are frustrated when they face such problems in the interior places. So a suitable place must be chosen in the important inter-islands namely Rangat, Mayabunder, Diglipur, Neil, Havelock, Wandoor, Chidiatappu etc. and small hotels, rest houses, guest houses, youth hostels, dormitory accommodations preferably with first floor constructed which will suit both domestic tourists and foreign tourists who are at middle level and rich level. As far as the form of ownership is concerned, the A & N Administration may invite the private investors to construct such small accommodation under the overall control of the tourism department in all such administrative matters namely fixing the tariff, provision of facilities, etc.

Another development has been noticed in the growth of tourism industry in these islands. That is the arrival of group tourists and family tourists is more than 10 - 30 persons. Sometimes this number goes beyond 75 also consisting of number of families. They would like to stay in a family type of accommodation. That is big room with kitchen facilities where they would like to cook according to their choice of taste, convenience and homely atmosphere. Once, about 60 persons (employees) came from B H E L of Thiruchirapalli, Tamil Nadu who asked for such accommodation by expressing their willingness that they wanted to stay for more days if such accommodation was available. This form of accommodation will be heartily welcomed by both the tourists i.e Domestic and Foreign. While making such accommodation, care must be taken to choose the place which should be near the bank, bus terminus, post office, taxi stand, market etc.

OFF-SEASON PROBLEMS

As is already mentioned, the best season for the tourist is from the October to mid of April and the season from mid of April to September is not much favourable for the tourists. In particular, May, June and July are very acute months when the number of tourists is very low. The lodges, hotels and other accommodations are not even 50% occupied during this season. Since there are no private hotels/ accommodations in the inter islands, this problem is not visible to others. Once if the tourism industry is grown, this problem will be obvious, needing a separate treatment. To attract more number of tourists even in this season, the tourism department, hotel owners, lodge owners etc. may calculate the concessional tariff and benefits on the basis of principles of marginal costing and announce the same. These concessions may be in the form of :

1. Discount during the off-season periods.
2. Meals on no profit and no loss basis.
3. Concessions if any tourist stays for more than 5-6 days.
4. Charging tariff for single tourist though they are more than two or three.
5. Family tourists' concession.
6. Sight Seeing/City Tour may be provided freely by the hotel owners if the tourists stay for more than 5-6 days
7. The accommodation owners may declare that the halls and even big rooms are available for the conference, seminars, discussions, talks etc. at concessional rates so that the institution, located nearby and even nearby islands, would be using it with some prestige.

So it is suggested that in Port Blair city the accommodation may be provided to the toutists during this off season at a discount of 50% and in the inter-islands the accommodations may be provided at a discount of 30%.

AIR/SHIP FARE

Another difficulty, facing the tourists, is intolerable air fare and ship fare. Very recently the ship fare as well as air fare have been increased. Even the tourists have expressed such problems. Major part of their total spending goes only for transport and that too while coming from one point to another point i.e. Chennai - Port Blair, Calcutta - Port Blair, Visakkapatnam - Port Blair. This increasing fare discourages the tourists to come to these islands and hence the tourism industry does not come up. Tourism in mainland flourishes becasue the transport cost is very low. To travel even 2000 Kms. the tourists hardly spend Rs. 200 - 500. So they would like to spend more and more on other shopping items etc. with an intention to stay more days. But in island tourism, a tourist spends Rs 10,000 - 30000 only on transport just for to and from charges. They are unable to go around the city and spend less because they have to keep another large sum to go back to the mainland. Moreover, the A & N islands is one of the important organs of our mainland of India like North Eastern Hill Regions. There people fly at a very low rate covering almost the same distance. So it is suggested that the air-fare and ship-fare may be reduced by adopting the technique of marginal costing by merging a marginal margin with the fare. During the off season, a 40% discount may be given to the tourists in order to attract more number.

TRANSPORT SERVICE

Foreign and Domestic tourists visit these islands by taking leave or with some tight programme schedule. It is quite normal that they may face language problem since they come from different parts of the country/world. Hence what they do, generally, is that they book / reserve the tickets for their modes of travel in advance and even they book for hotels and other accommodations. But the sudden change of shipping and flight schedule, diversion of ships, cancellation of ships, non arrival of flight from mainland, sudden strikes etc. are the dangerous factors contributing a lot of tension to the tourists. This is because all bookings, reservations of tickets and hotels, accommodation etc. will go waste and moreover, they have to stay in mainland till they get their further reservation, if there is a delay on the part of the tourists due to the reasons mentioned above.

It is understood from the discussion with the tourists leaving for Chennai/Calcutta next day that they would like to stay for some more days in these islands but due to the uncertainty of shipping schedule, they leave the islands so early. Hence it is suggested to have a regular transport services i.e both Air Service and Ship Service between the Islands and Mainland at the present situation, without any change or hindrance etc.

INTRODUCTION OF ISLAND AIR SERVICE

At present the A & N Administration is having a separate Shipping Department with a large number of employees. It is having 2 passenger cum cargo ships, 2 cargo ships plying between mainland and islands. As per the available information the Adrninistration grants concession, subsidies and bounties to the Shipping Authorities. It is suggested that the A & N Administration may purchase two Aircrafts(Very New) without any meaningless agreement as happened in the case of the M V Akbar and the same may be operated between Island - Mainland - Island on no profit and no loss basis. Two round trips each to Chennai and Ca1cutta with a modified fare are suggested. The proposed timings may be as under :

Port Blair - Chennai

Trip	Departure from Port Balir	Arrival at Chennai
I	04.00 a m	06.00 a m
II	04.00 p m	06.00 p m

Chennai - Port Blair

Trip	Departure from Chennai	Arrival at Port Blair
I	7.00 am	9.00 am
II	7.00 pm	9.00 pm

Port Blair - Calcutta

Trip	Departure from Port Blair	Arrival at Calcutta
I	5.00 am	7.00 am
II	5.00 pm	7.00 pm

Calcutta - Port Blair

Trip	Departure from Calcutta	Arrival at Port Blair
I	8.00 am	10.00 am
II	8.00 pm	10.00 pm

If the Island Air Service is started, it will be a solution for many transport problems, a booster dose to the island tourism, and will be gracious to the tourists and other public from the Administration, and bestover of booms. It is suggested that a high power committee, consisting of experts, academicians, technicians, excluding politicians may be constituted to invite the offer from the private investors to operate such Island Air Service, if Administration so desires.

PROVISION OF HEALTH SERVICE

Still the image of "Kalapani Andaman" in the minds of some public in the mainland dominates and hence it forces them to think about mosquitos, malaria fever etc. Only very few people understand about this lush green marigold sun paradise. Hardly one or two cases of malaria are found and it makes a name as such. So it is suggested that health department of these islands should take all steps to eradicate malaria, Andaman Fever etc. by taking proper steps and as a challenge. Merely going to every house and giving some suggestions will not solve the problem and the purpose. The department should find out cause and effect and try to cut at the root cause. The important tourists enter like Port Blair city, Wandoor, Chiddiatappu, Rangat, Mayabunder etc. It is suggested that 24 hrs. health service should be provided to the tourists. Serving with smile is absolutely necessary in order to develop the Industry.

INSTRUCTIONS TO THE PRIVATE ACCOMMODATIONS

Tourists are very much particular about the places of stay. During the tourist season, really the tourists face problems due to non- availability of accommodation in the city and in the inter-islands. Though they wish to stay in a costly hotel they are forced to take some cheap accommodation where there is no laundry, lavoratory, mosquito net, proper ventilation, protected drinking water facilities and are in bad hygienic conditions. These types of accommodation will make the tourists frustrated and indirectly force them to have a bad opinion about this destination. So it is suggested that the Tourism Department must have a regular checking of all accommodations whether the basic facilities are provided with proper hygienic conditions or not.

CONSTRUCTION OF PUBLIC TOILETS

At present, in A & N islands there is no 'pay and use' toilet. Public toilet facilitiy is totally absent at important beaches like Carbyn's Cove, Wandoor etc., and parks like Gandhi park and Marina park etc. The road sides and other important place are made dirty due to the want of public toilet especially during the festival time. So it is suggested to construct public toilets with the provision of maintenance at important places of the city, important beaches, grounds and parks.

CONSTRUCTION OF MILE STONES AND PILLARS

A & N Administration may immediately conduct an overall survey in order to fix the mile stones, concrete pillars, sign pillars and plates etc. Each road, street, lane, footpath, village etc. should be rightly and necessarily named. In some islands, places are termed as ' Theen Number' & 'Char Number' etc. Such names may be replaced by some freedom fighters' names. For every 3 Kms. tourist map, made out of concrete plates, of that or nearby locality should be fixed so that the tourists do not face any problem.

PROMOTING LOCAL INDUSTRIES

As A & N islands is very famous for the shell made items, wood made items etc., the amount spent by the tourists on shopping directly stimulates the local industries and handicrafts. Tourists visit these islands happily and purchase the locally made handicraft items as a symbol of visit to Andamans. They even present these items to their kith and kin, relatives and friends, as a sign/mark of their love and affection with a proud thought that this is made in Andamans. Such purchases by the tourists increase the total efficiency or quality of the local artisans, employment opportunities, the revenue to the islands and economic development as a whole. So it becomes necessary to know the main items or products which are purchased by the tourists, both Domestic and Foreign. In A & N islands, there are no silk saree industires, iron industries etc. So the scope of shopping for the tourists is limited to the shell made items, wood made items and forest products. Some sellers charge extraordinary high price from the tourists and such activities of some unscrupulous sellers disturb the shopping behaviour of the tourists and thereby the growth of tourism industry. The tourism department or the A & N Administration may calculate the cost of production of the items which are eagerly purchased by the tourists by adopting the technique of marginal costing technique and ask the sellers to sell only at that price fixed by the Administration. So it is suggested that the A & N Administration may have some control over such local industries by creating a special cell who will look after price control, quality control etc. of the products in which the tourists are interested. Local industries may be guaranteed for the supply of raw materials and purchase of final products by the A & N Administration/ tourism department.

PROTECTING THE SOCIO-CULTURAL LIFE

The socio cultural life of the people of A & N islands is unpolluted, highly valued and need of this hour at present situation, and just can not be compared with any other region or country. While planning for tourism, care must be taken to protect the socio-cultural life style of these islands. This is because, some religious heads, politicians from different parts of mainland through their talks, create some tension among the people of these islands. The department of tourism should come forward to verify such activites. Talks, speeches by such people on the open ground is not a problem but the way in which they talk and speak which are spliting the people is the problem and that should not be allowed. Hence it is suggested that the clearance from the Tourism Department for such speeches, talks should be made compulsory. Tourism Department should, before granting such permission, take note of their proposed speech and talk and verify them so that it should not affect the growth of tourism industry and should not damage the socio-cultural life of the people which is one of the important tourism resources.

NEW TOURISM ROUTES FROM ABROAD

A & N islands is surrounded by Thailand, Burma, Vietnam, Combodia, Malaysia, Singapore etc. Air distance between A & N islands and the nearby countries is given below. A tourist who wishes to visit the lush green paradise has to travel a long route or distance by adopting different formalities of international rules. For example, a tourist from Bangkok wishes to visit A & N islands, he has to travel from Bangkok to Calcutta/Chennai and from Calcutta/Chennai to A & N islands. That is, he has to travel almost about 3500 kms. to reach these islands whereas the distance between Bangkok and Port Blair is just 544 kms. The tourist has to spend for airfare to travel for 6000-7000 kms. to and fro. If there is

Table 9.1
Air Distance between A & N Islands and Nearby Countries

	A & N Islands	Countries	Distance (in Kms.)
1.	Great Nicobar	Atjeh	135
2.	Car Nicobar	Phuket	378
3.	Port Blair	Rangoon	422
4.	Port Blair	Phuket	447
5.	Port Blair	Bangkok	544
6,	Port Blair	Penang	655
7.	Carnicobar	Penang	558
8.	Port Blair	Cox's Bazar	668
9.	Port Blair	Kaula.Lampur	817
10.	Port Blair	Singapore	1011
11.	Carnicobar	Singapore	897

Source: Tourism Department, Port Blair.

a direct route to A & N islands, he travels only about 1000 kms. for to and fro and so the expenses come down. In the same manner, a tourist from Japan has to come to Delhi and from Delhi to Calcutta/Chennai and from Calcutta/ Chennai to A & N islands. If there is a direct route to Andaman from Japan, from Bangkok and so on, the tourists particulary the foreign tourists find it very easy to come to Andaman by saving a lot of amount which can be spent by the tourists on shopping at Port Blair. The tourists from abroad do not stay for many days and do not spend much in Andamans because the major portion of their expenses goes to transport part. So it is suggested that the Govt. of India may take steps to put the A & N islands on any two international routes as proposed below :

1. Bangkok - Port Blair - Chennai
2. Malasiya - Port Blair - Chennai
3 Chennai - Port Blair - Malasiya
4. Chennai - Port Blair - Bangkok

If such proposed routes are opened, the A & N islands will attract more number of tourists from abroad, Since the distance to be travelled would be reduced by the extent of 5/6th i.e 85 % & the travelling expenses also would be reduced to the same extent which will facilitate the tourists to stay for more days by spending more in A & N islands and thereby our country will earn a lot of foreign exchange.

DISPOSAL OF SEWAGE

The Port Blair city, the only thickly populated area in this territory has to be beautified. The first hindrance to the beautification is the stagnant sewage at important places of the city. Gutters do not have free flow of sewage water. Channels of drainage have to be properly designed and constructed accordingly. Nature cleans the whole territory by way of heavy rain. But some senseless persons throw waste, empty bottles, body of the dead animals etc. into the gutters which results in the blocking of sewage. The A &

N Administration may announce through AIR and the Daily Telegramme News Paper that the people should not throw such items into the channels of sewage. It may also announce the punishment if they do so. Dust-bins, litter-boxes are to be placed at every 100 meters and regularly the dust-bins and litter-boxes are to be cleared.

RESERVATION FACILITY

As far as the sea transport between these islands and the mainland is concerned, the reservation facility may be made available in the mainland also. The S C I and the Directorate of Shipping of A & N islands may recruit some agents at the places far away from Chennai, Calcutta and Visakkapatnam. For example, if a tourist of Kannyakumari wishes to come to these islands he/she has to contact the SCI office, Chennai for availability of tickets, shipping programme and the SCI office or Directorate of Shipping, Port Blair for the reservation. If the reservation facility is available in the mainland itself and the agents are nearby, it will facilitate the tourist to take quick decision and action. So it is suggested that the shipping authorities may appoint some of their agents at different places, suitably away from the Chennai, Calcutta and Visakkapatnam.

MORE ISLANDS FOR FOREIGN TOURISTS

At present very limited islands have been opened for foreign tourists. And the foreign tourists are not allowed to stay during night hours in any island. It is suggested that more number of islands may be opened for these tourists.

LIGHTING FACILITY FOR BEACHES

Lighting facilities may be provided for the roads which lead to important beaches like Carbyn'scove, Wandoor, Chidiaṭappu etc. and also in the beaches itself. Seating facilities with the decorated shades may be constructed at the centre of the beaches. The central place which contains the proposed chairs and tables may be fenced and maintained neatly, and be provided with illuminated designed colour lights. Regular checking must be made to check the imrnoral activities.

DRINKING WATER

Soft water is another major problem in this territory. Water for drinking is a vital important resource. At present there is only one dam which supplies water for drinking and it is- Dhannikari Dam. But another tank called Thilthaman Tank which was used as a source for drinking water is, at present, used for water sports. But the water sports can be played in any waveless sea water also. Growing necessity of water, due to the increase in population, for drinking purposes compels the Administration to find out different means for the storage of rain water. So it is suggested that the Thilthaman Tank should also be used for drinking purposes and the water sports may be stopped.

REMOVAL OF FALLEN TREES

The places like Chidiatappu, Wandoor etc. are the fine beaches. But they are shrouded by the fallen trees. They have a good quality of soil but the hidden timber nails of fallen trees hinder the free walk of the tourists on beaches. These beaches are not at all looked after by the A & N Administration. These fallen trees have economic value. If they are auctioned, the Administration can get a good amount of income which can be utilised for the development of the beaches. So it is suggested that the Administration may take immediate necessary steps to remove the fallen trees from the beaches in order to bring back the beauty of the beautiful beaches.

CABLE CARS/ROPE-WAYS

Cable cars/rope-ways is an interesting attraction to the tourists. This is the best source of entertainment. At present such cars/rope-ways are totally absent in the A & N islands. If this source is provided, it will be like adding honey to the mixed fruit juice. The following places/points are suggested to instal the cable cars/rope-ways:

1. Haddo to Bambooflat
2. Haddo to Chidiatappu
3. Mount Harriet to Ross Island
4. Marina Park to Ross Island
5. Wandoor to Redskin/Jolly Bouy
6. Carbyn's cove to Ross Island

BUSES AND BUS TERMINUS

The number of buses must be increased. Since A&N islands is a multi-lingual society, the name plates of the destinations should be written in at least four languages namely, Tamil, Hindi, Bengali and English in all the passenger buses irrespective of the ownership. Instructions may be issued to follow this system strictly and regularly. One more bus terminus is to be constructed near school-line. Buses for the places outside the Municipal limit may be operated from this proposed bus terminus i.e Long route and very long route buses are to be operated from the proposed bus terminus.

ACCOMMODATION AT MAINLAND

Tourist accommodation near the harbour and the airport may be constructed at Chennai, Calcutta and Visakkpatanam which may contain more number of dormitory type beds. This is in order to facilitate the stay of the tourists and visitors of A & N islands. The tourists may be allowed to stay for a period of 10 days depending upon the rush. No tourist should be disturbed with the popular and meaningless words like "VIP is coming, so please vacate". It is suggested that the so called disturbing VIPs may not be allowed to stay in the proposed guest houses and even if they are allowed, they should be treated at par with the tourists so far as they stay in the accommodation.

POSSIBILITY OF FREE PORT

These green islands are located on the world maritime route. Particularly the Great Nicobar is very near the route. Though not all, at least the Great Nicobar Islands may be taken for the consideration of declaration of the opening of Free Port. It is strongly believed/expected/predicted by the author that if the island is declared as Free Port, the A&N Administration will get a lot of revenue in terms of foreign exchange. But this issue is to be properly studied by taking all factors into consideration. So it is suggested to appoint a separate project committee, excluding the political parties, to study the issue.

OTHER SUGGESTIONS

1. The floating hotels may be constructed in the Port Blair city. For this purpose any scraped shipping vessel may be purchased and used.

2. A&N Administration may invite private sector to run 'pay and use' toilets, bathrooms etc. at important places such as bus teminuses, existing as well as proposed, parks, beaches, bazars, taluk head quarters etc. The tourism department may be entrusted the work of supervision in order to check the immoral activities.

3. Facility of getting the tickets both for ship and flight by post may be provided both in the mainland and in the islands. Necessary arrangements may be made either by the SCI, Directorate of Shipping or Indian Airlines or by tourism department.

4. The Shipping authorities may publish the sailing programme at least, one month in advance in the leading and well circulated daily newspaper which can facilitate the tourists to make their programme well in advance.

5. Adequate inter-islands transport facilities may be provided by the A&N Administration in order to facilitate the tourists to fulfil their programme as per their pre-planned schedule. Regular and adequate inter-island transport facillity can be a booster dose to the tourism industry which is at its infant stage.

6. A&N Administration should fix the standard price and standard quality for the various food items. This should be strictly followed by all the hotels, guest houses, canteens and hostels etc. Proper feed back should be maintained for the quality control. The standard price should be acceptable by even a lower income bracketed tourists.

To conclude, the A&N islands is a very beautiful tourists destination. It is evident from the survey that the tourists have high opinions about the tourism attractions of A&N islands. The suggestions for the tourism planning in these islands have been offered which are based on the problems, facing the industry and the possiblity of development of the tourism industry in this lush green paradise.

It is easy to give suggestions, to recommend schemes etc. but the feasibility of their implementation should be taken into consideration, particularly from the point of view of finance. By and large, all suggestions, made above, are economically viable and feasible and worth trying. The A&N islands has vast potential resources to be exploited for the development of tourism industry and it is upto the planners and the A & N Administration, Govt. of India, Development authorities to provide more tourism facilities so that the tourism industry will grow to a greater extent which will also contribute to the development of Indian Economy. For that, there should be a wide publicity and advertisement about A&N islands, a provision to show the visitors/tourists a glimpse of the socio cultural life of this Mini India (A & N Islands) and to make them feel that the A&N islands is the place for national integration in the world. Popular lectures and shows should be arranged in these islands for the tourists who have come to A&N islands and in the mainland for the tourists who are in the mainland to highlight the value and importance of these islands, and the vital role played by the places of interest. What is required is a bold decision by avoiding any to vitalise tourism with the long term benefits in view in A&N Islands. All these facilities would make the visit of the tourists to these golden sunny Bay Islands both memorable and happy.

BIBLIOGRAPHY

Acharya, Ram, "Civil Aviation and Tourism Administration in India"—A Study in Management,National Publishing House,New Delhi, 1978.

Agarwall, H.N., " Reproductive Life of Onge Women", *Vanyajati,* Vol. XV No. 3 1967.

Agarwal, H.N.", The Social effects of Tourism", *Current Anthropology* ,13, 1972.

Akthar, Javaid," Tourism Management in India", Ashish Publishing House, New Delhi, 1990.

Anand. M.M., "Tourism and Hotel Industry in India", Prentice Hall of India, New Delhi, 1976.

Andaman & Nicobar Administration, Jan Jathi Vikas Samity, "Retrival from the Precipice", Port Blair, 1977.

Andaman & Nicobar Administration, "Gazetteer", A & N Islands, Calcutta, 1939.

Ayyar, T.G.N., " Meet Our Onges", A & N Information, Port Blair, 1957.

Basu, D.N., " A Linguistic Introduction to Andamanese", *Bulletin of the Department of Anthropology,* 1 (2), 1952.

Basu, Bada Kumar, "The ASI A & N Islands Tribal Series", Seegul Books, Calcutta, 1990.

Batra, K.L., " Problems and Prospects of Tourism", Printwell, Jaipur, 1989.

Balsdon, JPVD., " Life and Leisure in Ancient Rome", Bodley Head, London, 1966

Banerjee, S.K., Das, A.K. and Raha, M.K., "Lodha Settlement: An Evaluation", *Bulletin of Cultural Research Institute,* Calcutta, 1964.

Bhatia, A.K., "International Tourism: Fundamental and Practices", Sterling Publisers, New Delhi, 1978.

Bhatia, A.K.," Tourism in India: History and Development", Sterling Publishers, New Delhi, 1978

Blair, Archibaid, "Survey of the Andamans", Selection from the Records of the Govt. of India.

Bouyden, John N., "Tourism and Development", Cambridge University, Press, London, 1976.

Bonnington, M.C.C., " Report on the Andamans in Census of India 1931", A Govt. of India Central Publication Branch, Calcutta, 1931.

Bonnington, M.C.C., "Census of India, 1931, Andaman and Nicobar Island", Parts 1 and 2, 1932.

Bose, S.C., " Source of Ganga", In Mountain and Rivers of India, (Ed. Chaterjee S P) National Committee for Geography, Calcutta, 1968.

Bose, S.C, "Economy of the Onge Society", *Man in India* 44: 298-310, 1964.

Burkart and Medlik, "Tourism—Past, Present and Future", Heinemann, London, 1974.

Burns, Edward M. & Others, " World Civilisation: Their History and Culture", Norton & Co., New York, 1974.

Burkert, A.J., "The Management of Tourism", Heinemann, London, 1975.

Butler, R.W., "The Social Implications of Tourism Development", *Tourism Research* 2, 2. 1974.

Charles, Kaiser Jr. and Helber, Larry E., " Tourism—Planning and Development", C B I Publications, Boston, Massachusetts, 1971.

Chak, B.L., "Andman and Nicobar Islands, Ministry of Information and Broadcasting", Govt. of India, New Delhi, 1967.

Chalder, N., "The Environment Game", Panther Publications, London, 1960

Chatterjee, N.N., "Status of Indian Tourism", *Yojana*, Planning Commission of India, New Delhi, Vol. XIX, No. 11 1975.

Ciprani, L., "The Andaman Islanders", Weidenfield and Nicolson, London, 1966

Chopra, Suhita, "Tourism and Development in India", Asish Publishing House, New Delhi, 1991.

Dutta, P.C., "The Great Andamanese: Past and Present", Anthropological Survey of India, Govt. of India, Calcutta, 1978.

Das, Manoj, "A Tourist Paradise", Sterling Publishing House, New Delhi, 1985.

Dass, S.T., "Andaman and Nicobar Islands (from Tradition and Modernity", Sagar Publications, New Delhi, 1982.

English Tourist Board (Planning and Research), "Planning for Tourism" in England, London.

Edmunds, " Environmental Administration", McGraw Hill, New York, 1973.

Gupta, Vijay Kumar, " Tourism in India", Gian, Delhi, 1987.

Ghosh, "Census of India 1951, Andaman and Nicobar Islands", Port Blair 17 (Parts 1 & 2), 1955.

Joshi M.C., "Census of India 1971: A & N Islands", Port Blair, Series 23 (Part V A) 1976.

Jayal, N.D. and M. Mohan, "Conservation, Tourism and Mountaineering in the Himalayas", Neeraj Publications, Dehradun, 1986.

Kaul, R.N., "Dynamics of Tourism—A Trilogic", Sterling Publications, New Delhi, 1985.

Krishnathry, S.M., "Brief Resume of Activities of the Andaman Adim Jan Jathi Vikas", Vikas Samiti, Port Blair, 1974.

Kloss, C .B., "Andaman and Nicobars Roprint", Vivek Publishing House, New Delhi, 1971.

Kayasatha, S.L., "Transportation and Communication in the Himalayas", Beas Basin, Varanasi, NGJI, Vol. VI Pt. 2 1960

Khanna, S.D., "Report", The Hotel Review and Survey Committee, Ministry of Tourism, Delhi, 1968.

Kumar, H.L., "Personnel Management in Hotel and Catering Industry", Metropolitan, New Delhi, 1986.

Maneet Kumar, "Tourism Today: An Indian Perspective", Kanishka Publishing House, New Delhi, 1992.

Man, E.H., "Aboriginals Inhabitants of Andaman Islands", *J R 12,* 109-116, 1883.

Mann, R.S., "The Bay Islanders", Institute of Social Research and Applied Anthropology, Calcutta, 1978.

Malhotra, O.P., " Tribal Education in A & N Islands", S. Chand & Co. Ltd., New Delhi, 1986.

Mishra, R.P., Acharya, Ram and Sharma, "World Tourism", Delta International, Jaipur, 1981.

Muni Lal, "Haryana: On High Road to the Prosperity", Vikas Publishing House, Delhi, 1974.

National Action Plan for Tourism, Govt. of India, Ministry of Civil Aviation and Tourism, New Delhi, 1996.

N C A E R, "Cost Benefit Study of Tourism", NCAER, New Delhi, 1975.

Negi, J.M.S., "Tourism and Hotellering", Gitanjali Publishing House, New Delhi, 1982.

Nigam, R.C., "The Onge of Little Andaman—Their Settlement and Population", *Vanyajati,* Vol.10. No. 2

Pandit, T.N., "The Economy of the Onge—Case Study of a Hunting Gathering Tribe" (Unpublished) 1978.

Pandit, T.N., "Aborigins of the Bay Islands"—A Review, A & N Information, Port Blair, 1971.

Sen, Prabhat Kumar, "Land and the People of Andaman", Government of India, New Delhi, 1962.

Pranab Ganguly, "Physical Anthropology of Nicobarese", Anthropological Survey of India, Govinda, 1963.

Pandit, T.N., "The Sentinalese"—The ASI A & N Tribals Series, Seagul Books, Calcutta, 1990.

Rajavel N., "Problems and Prospects of Trade, Commerce and Industry in A & N Islands", Kumaun University, Nainital Ph. D. Thesis (Unpublished), 1990.

Rao, Prakash, "Death in an Onge Family", A & N Information, Port Blair, 1960.

Rabinson, H., "Geography of Tourism", McDonold & Evans Ltd, London, 1976

Roy, P.B., "India—A Hand Book of Travel", Saturday Mail, Narendrapur, 1980.

Selvam, M., "Tourism Industry in India", Himalaya Publishing House, New Delhi, 1978.

Seth, Prem Nath, "Successful Tourism Planning and Management", Cross Setia Publications, New Delhi, 1978.

Singh, S.N., "Geography of Tourism and Recreation", Inter India Publications, New Delhi, 1986.

Singh, T.V., "Tourism and Tourist Industry in UP", New Height, Delhi, 1975.

Tamta, B.R., "A & N Islands", National Book Trust, New Delhi, 1992.

Index